JUDITH B

D1475891

M·O·N·E·Y

G·U·I·D·E

F O R

CHRISTIAN WOMEN

A PROFESSIONAL FINANCIAL CONSULTANT GIVES ADVICE ON INVESTING, SAVING BORROWING, LENDING AND OTHER ASPECTS OF MANAGING YOUR MONEY PROFITABLY

Regal Books
A Division of GL Publications
Ventura, California, U.S.A.

Dedication

For Cristin and Torri

Published by Regal Books
A Division of GL Publications
Ventura, California 93006
Printed in U.S.A.

The author and publisher specifically disclaim any liability, loss, or risk, personal or otherwise, which is incurred as a consequence, directly or indirectly, from the use and application of any of the contents of this work. Furthermore, questions relevant to the practice of law or accounting should be addressed to a member of those professions.

Formerly published under the title *Faith and Savvy, Too!*

Library of Congress Cataloging-in-Publication Data applied for

1 2 3 4 5 6 7 8 9 10 / 95 94 93 92 91

Rights for publishing this book in other languages are contracted by Gospel Literature International (GLINT) foundation. GLINT also provides technical help for the adaptation, translation, and publishing of Bible study resources and books in scores of languages worldwide. For further information, contact GLINT, Post Office Box 488, Rosemead, California, 91770, U.S.A., or the publisher.

Any omission of credits or permission granted is unintentional. The publisher requests documentation for future printings.

Contents

Foreword

How grateful we readers should be that Judith Briles, already a celebrated author in the secular market, has taken the time to write a book addressed to the financial needs of today's Christian woman. So much of what we read is directed at personal improvement and Bible study; it's exciting to have a helpful handbook for those of us who need instruction in financial planning, or who suddenly find ourselves heads of households we don't know how to financially manage.

When I first heard Judith speak at a National Speakers Association convention, I was impressed with her communication skills and her obvious wealth of knowledge on things that were just letters of the alphabet to me: IRA, IRS, CD, AGI, ESOP. She was able to explain terms and taxes in a way I could understand. As we became better acquainted, I suggested she come to our CLASS (Christian Leaders and Speakers Seminar), and even though she was already a professional speaker, she came in humility to learn more.

My most indelible memory of Judith was in the final hours of our three-day CLASS, when she stood up and challenged the attendees to support CLASS ministries, because what they received was worth so much more than what they had paid for. That was a one-of-a-kind statement, and I will never forget her for making it.

I suggested to Judith she write a practical financial book for Christian women, but because of her complex career as financial planner, president of her own company, columnist, board member of *Executive Female* magazine, author of five books and noted seminar leader and keynote speaker, it seemed an impossible dream. But she did it, and today *The Money Guide for Christian Women* is available for you to learn, to know and to grow in the knowledge of money matters.

It's great to have faith in the Lord's provision for our futures, for He holds us accountable for what we do with our talents at hand.

Florence Littauer

Preface

This book almost didn't get written. At least, it almost didn't get a publisher. The reason: mostly tunnel vision. The key decision makers were men—many of whom felt my writing may be too sophisticated for today's Christian woman. Salesmen worried the book might be difficult to sell if it became known I was an elder in my church. Statements that, at first, made me laugh, made me later feel deep pain.

As the concept was gelling, I visited many of the Christian bookstores near my home. Most were lacking in any kind of money management books. The books they did carry were written by men. The very few I found authored by women did not have much depth.

I saw a need. An exciting challenge loomed. I felt called to undertake the mission of writing a legible, realistic and practical money book designed specifically for the Christian woman. And that I did!

The Money Guide for Christian Women is your book. It was written especially for you!

Acknowledgments

No book gets written without lots of help. Mine is no exception.

My family was and is always there; they are my biggest rooters. Thanks John, Shelley, Sheryl, Dave, Frankie, Joyce, Bill, Terry, Joan, Doc and Louise.

Thanks, too, to my church family at Valley Presbyterian Church in Portola Valley, California, and to my new friends at Gospel Light, Mary, Connie, Linda, and old friend Keith, who believed in my vision.

To my new friends John, Shirin and Marilyn who always encouraged me to push on; to Louie and Jo, who unscrambled all the dictation, and to Keenan, who became my new right hand, many thanks.

In February of 1984 I met a remarkable woman, Florence Littauer. She's an inspiration to all who come in contact with her. I am honored to have her as my friend and supporter. With her introduction, I met Dick, whose enthusiasm became the catalyst for this book. And through him I met Roy and Pat, who are all very much part of the success of this project.

Thank you all.

JB

CHAPTER ONE

Finances, Females and Faith: How They Fit Together

This book is about money. It's also about women. Specifically Christian women. To many, these are glaring contradictions in terms, and that's why this book is necessary. Even in our advanced society women have not earned strong respect or recognition as money managers.

Ironically, we have proven we can do almost anything else a man can do. Not only have we asserted ourselves as doctors, lawyers, merchants and chiefs, we have become "superwomen," balancing careers and family in the most remarkable way. But in probably one of the single most important area of American society—financial savvy—many of us remain woefully uninformed and uncertain.

To be ignorant of money workings is to remain a powerless outsider to an enormously significant aspect of daily life. By failing to participate in long-term money management, we have abdicated our power and right to be financially aware and independent.

WHY NOT WOMEN AND MONEY?

A woman may be an expert in any field from science to the arts, but we still don't know what to do with our salaries. Instead of thinking about investment programs and money management, we depend on parents, husbands or friends to take care of our money matters. We forget that other people make mistakes too. Worse, they sometimes die or

---

Since the financial world has been dominated by the more dependable, objective, deductive, left-brain reasoning of males, women have not been taken seriously.

---

become disabled or are lost through divorce. They may not always be there for us. We are satisfied with the safety and ease of savings accounts, letting a professional, our friendly banker, be our guide. We forget that bankers have vested interests of their own, that inflation often runs higher than bank interest rates or that bankers, too, make mistakes.

It doesn't help that somehow society still views money management as unfeminine. A woman who actively pursues money management is deemed aggressive and pushy. Even before girls grow up to be wives and mothers, parents and teachers tend to discourage them from taking an interest in money and numbers. They also discourage them from a more elementary financial necessity—the willingness to take risks. The penalties for mischief or adventurous misbehavior tend to be far greater for girls than for boys, who are expected to be more aggressive and daring.

Another deterrent has been that women are traditionally "right-brain" thinkers. Psychologists tell us that the
right side of the brain tends to control passion, intuition,
dreams and feelings. A woman is more apt to act from
instinct than from the strictly rational, logical "left-brain"
mode more dominant in men. The right-brain thinker is
more creative, sometimes more general, definitely less
predictable, always more subjective.

Since the financial world has been dominated by the
more dependable, objective, deductive, left-brain reasoning of males, women have not been taken seriously. Only
recently have credit cards been issued in a woman's name
alone, and even today, some banks consider women
"unfit" for large-scale dealings.

Society, at last, is changing, and the money mystique is
breaking down. We are all realizing that the short-term
skills of family finances are not so different from the long-
term skills of financial planning. In some cases, women
may actually have an advantage over men in the money
game. After all, we have shopped for years, and the same
skills that help us choose the best goods in a market can be
applied to the stock exchange.

Society tends to undermine our rights and abilities to
participate in long-term financial management. No wonder
we lack confidence and shy away from strategy-making.
But even the Bible acknowledges that women should
"work happily together" with man (Rom. 12:16) and that
"Two can accomplish more than twice as much as one, for
the results can be much better" (Eccles. 4:9).

It's time women add their unique genius to the money
game. "Praise her for the many fine things she does.
These good deeds of hers shall bring her honor and recognition from even the leaders of the nations," says Prov-

erbs 31:31. That ability and recognition cannot stop in the home or office.

Women have shown we can make money; now we must realize the importance of managing it as well. Too long have we worked for our money, letting it manage us. We must now make our money work for us. Women belong in money management.

Financial savvy, then, is important for us as women. It is also important for us as Christians. As Christian women,

---

Money is a means, not an end in itself, and money can give us the security and freedom to pursue our Christian values and put our faith in action.

---

we are interested in a life of involvement, awareness and fulfillment based on Christian faith. We trust that "God will provide," and we heed Paul's warning to Timothy, "And as Christ's soldier do not let yourself become tied up in worldly affairs, for then you cannot satisfy the one who has enlisted you in his army" (2 Tim. 2:4).

As Christians, we know our priorities begin with our principles. "People who long to be rich soon begin to do all kinds of wrong things to get money, things that hurt them and make them evil-minded and finally send them to hell itself. For the love of money is the first step toward all kinds of sin. Some people have even turned away from God because of their love for it, and as a result have pierced themselves with many sorrows" (1 Tim. 6:9,10). We may long to be rich, but it's not for the riches themselves, but rather for what we can do with those riches:

how they will enable us to enrich our lives and the lives of others in greater ways.

MONEY: A MEANS TO AN END

This book, then, is about using money, not loving money. Money is a means, not an end in itself, and money can give us the security and freedom to pursue our Christian values and put our faith in action. "The good man's earnings advance the cause of righteousness," says Proverbs 10:16.

Proper stewardship and management of those earnings are equally important in the service of God. Jesus told us that He came so that we may have life and have it more abundantly: "My purpose is to give life in all its fullness" (John 10:10). Abundance is emotional, spiritual, intellectual—and material. Financial savvy is good stewardship and thus implicit in our faith, and consistent with the biblical principles of planting, growing and reaping.

In the Old Testament, many of the practical instructions for successful living are included in Proverbs. Solomon supplements the teaching of the prophets with human wisdom and commonsense comments for day-to-day decisions. This book will use numerous quotes from Proverbs—and there are many—to illustrate God's teaching on money matters. And in the New Testament, through the parables, Jesus gives us practical instructions for living.

One important parable, the parable of the talents, has particular relevance for us in matters of financial stewardship. Its message runs throughout this book and underscores the fact that money, and what we do with it, matters to us as women, and as Christians.

Again, the Kingdom of Heaven can be illustrated by the story of a man going into another country, who called together his servants and loaned them money to invest for him while he was gone.

He gave $5,000 to one, $2,000 to another, and $1,000 to the last—dividing it in proportion to their abilities—and then left on his trip. The man who received the $5,000 began immediately to buy and sell with it and soon earned another $5,000. The man with $2,000 went right to work, too, and earned another $2,000.

But the man who received the $1,000 dug a hole in the ground and hid the money for safe-keeping.

After a long time their master returned from his trip and called them to him to account for his money. The man to whom he had entrusted the $5,000 brought him $10,000.

His master praised him for good work. "You have been faithful in handling this small amount," he told him, "so now I will give you many more responsibilities. Begin the joyous tasks I have assigned to you."

Next came the man who had received the $2,000, with the report, "Sir, you gave me $2,000 to use, and I have doubled it."

"Good work," his master said. "You are a good and faithful servant. You have been faithful over this small amount, so now I will give you much more."

Then the man with the $1,000 came and said, "Sir, I knew you were a hard man, and I was afraid you would rob me of what I earned, so I hid your money in the earth and here it is!"

But his master replied, "Wicked man! Lazy slave! Since you knew I would demand your profit, you should at least have put my money in the bank so I could have some interest. Take the money from this man and give it to the man with the $10,000. For the man who uses well what he is given shall be given more, and he shall have abundance. But from the man who is unfaithful, even what little responsibility he has shall be taken from him. And throw the useless servant out into outer darkness: there shall be weeping and gnashing of teeth." (Matt. 25:14-30).

As you read and use the following chapters, remember the parable of the talents, and let it be your guide.

CHAPTER TWO

The Four I's: Intuition, Involvement, Information, Identification

Financial savvy is primarily a matter of trusting yourself and realizing your own potential for money management. Housewives and mothers are involved in elementary money management tasks every day, though they may not be aware of that because they lack knowledge of the proper vocabulary.

Women are good at planning family finances. We may not always know the theory behind financial maneuvers, but when the tasks performed instinctively are placed in the proper context—which is one of the aims of this book—money begins to make sense.

Money sense begins with believing in yourself, in understanding that you, as a woman, have a unique ability to turn possibilities into realities. Financial savvy is not packaged in some masculine learned logic. It begins with your own intuitive insights. The Bible continually counsels the value of common sense:

Get the facts at any price, and hold on tightly to all the good sense you can get (Prov. 23:23).

Be strong! Be courageous! Do not be afraid of them! For the Lord your God will be with you. He will neither fail you nor forsake you (Deut. 31:6).

As God's messenger I give each of you God's warning: Be honest in your estimate of yourselves, measuring your value by how much faith God has given you. Just as there are many parts to our bodies, so it is with Christ's body. We are all parts of it, and it takes every one of us to make it complete, for we each have different work to do. So we belong to each other, and each needs all the others (Rom. 12:3-5).

INTUITION LEADS TO INVOLVEMENT

Financial savvy, then, contains large doses of intuition, or common sense. But even intuition needs to be based on information, which comes from involvement. And successful stewardship requires involvement. One kind of involvement is simply awareness—paying attention to what goes on around you.

Women are traditionally expert at shopping and finding bargains. The same skills that help us choose the best goods in a supermarket can be applied to the stock exchange and other markets.

For instance, some years ago, three friends and I noticed that coffee was becoming more and more expensive. We knew nothing that millions of other women shoppers didn't know. But instead of just knowing it, we noticed it. And we decided that increased prices meant coffee was becoming scarce. Supply must equal demand, therefore coffee must be becoming more valuable. My

---

The same skills that help us choose the best goods in a supermarket can be applied to the stock exchange and other markets.

---

friends and I pooled our resources, bought a coffee contract on the commodities market, and made more than $70,000 profit in a few months.

Our involvement in the evolving financial world made us aware of an opportunity. Our intuition and confidence made us act on it. Awareness of the marketplace, involvement in what was going on in the world, was the key to success. We were elated when we made so much money, not even realizing initially that we could make so much with our $5,000 investment. We were, however, totally aware that we could lose everything—all of our $5,000— if coffee didn't increase in value.

Another example of this kind of awareness involves a company named Pizza Time Theater. When I first visited one in 1981, I felt it offered an exciting opportunity to make money. The place was packed. The pizza wasn't terrific, but the action was. Here was an establishment catering to young families with children ages 4 to 11, providing supper plus entertainment. There was no other place like it at the time.

A call to a stockbroker revealed that Pizza Time Theater was a publicly owned company; I could purchase stock directly, if I chose to. However, I was also aware that if the Pizza Time concept worked as well as the initial encounter indicated, there would be several imitations. And eventually the intrigue of the concept would wear off.

Once you buy into a rapidly moving stock like Pizza Time, you should also determine when to sell. The day you go into a Pizza Time and find that there is not only an open table, but space around many of the games, it's time to sell!

If you'll commit to reading, or even just scanning the newspapers every day, a wealth of information will come your way. Repeated headlines may mean investment potential or opportunity.

OUTSIDERS' INFORMATION

And what about you? Do you use any cosmetics? Are you getting older? If you answered yes to either of the last two questions, there are a myriad of investment opportunities at your fingertips.

The next time you're in a drugstore, beauty or facial salon or the cosmetics department at your favorite department store, ask what brands are selling and why. The odds are that the responses you get are the same throughout the country. If you're from California, you'll soon learn, if you don't already know, that many trends begin in the Golden State. Trends also begin on the East Coast.

Probably the best newspaper coming out of California is the *Los Angeles Times*. It's available at many newsstands and airports around the country. Do yourself a favor and pick up a Sunday edition once in a while. Note the ads and articles in the *women's, style* and *living* sections. Big money is spent here and you don't have to pay for the promotions; just buy the paper.

If you'll commit to reading, or even just scanning the newspapers every day, a wealth of information will come your way. Repeated headlines may mean investment potential or opportunity.

Do you wonder what to do with your cash—how to get the best yield or return without increasing your risk? Simply by reading the newspaper—the two or three paragraph article (usually on Tuesdays) that tells you whether six-month treasury bill yields are up or down. If the yield goes up four weeks in a row, then move your funds to a money market fund or a 90-day treasury bill. Four weeks of increased rates is my signal that interest rates will continue to increase. In this position your funds will continue to reinvest at the higher rates.

On the other hand, if the treasury yield decreases four weeks in a row, move them to a 1-year treasury bill or one of the longer term money market funds. These funds report the average number of days they mature every Wednesday in the *Wall Street Journal*. Moving your money to these areas allows you to enjoy a higher interest rate than the funds that mature sooner.

If interest rates are up one week and down the next or in any combination in a four week period, stay put. No real change is developing.

To participate in treasury bills, you need a minimum of $10,000. If that is beyond your means, then the many money market funds will take care of you. In fact, some of the funds only invest in treasury obligations, but have a minimum buy-in of only a few hundred dollars. There is always something for everyone. Just ask.

Remember in 1986 when students were demonstrating against companies that did business with South Africa? The end result was that many of those companies closed their operations, and imports increased in value due to the perceived shortages. Gold was and is one of South Africa's primary commodities. When various sanctions were imposed, even when they were just a threat, the price per ounce increased almost 30 percent within a few months.

Could you have made money? Sure, by buying gold outright, buying shares in a gold mutual fund or stock or purchasing coins.

Inside information? Absolutely not—just information that is available through newspapers, magazines, radio and television.

THE REAL INSIDE SCOOP

Involvement and identification go hand in hand. Involvement also means keeping informed. This does not mean taking crash courses in securities law, Fannie Mae's or CPI implications. (We talk more about these later.) Nor does it mean reading the stock market report each day to check the status of 100 shares of your favorite stock. It does mean reading the newspapers. It means a commitment of 15 to 20 minutes a day to read the front page of your local paper, as well as the headlines and the first three or four paragraphs of each story in the business section. After a while you will recognize that reports of large lay-offs within a particular industry or field indicate a fall within that field. Stay away from related investments.

Similarly, dividend drops or store or office closings indicate trouble. On the other hand, a series of new hirings, or promotions, or the engagement of a larger advertising firm, all indicate business is on the move. After a while you will begin to read more analytically. Declining (or rising) interest rates, crop failures, devaluation of the dollar and the toppling of governments may all seem irrelevant to you on a day-to-day basis, but they *will* affect your investments.

It is not the daily stock market changes that will affect your stock. It is the underlying prevailing trends in population densities, housing and business preferences, tax advantages and real estate values.

I've said you don't need more than your daily newspaper to keep abreast of investment trends. Certainly it is unwise, not to mention downright confusing, to get caught up in the myriad investment newsletters, advice columns and brokers' "tips" that abound. But there are two sources outside of your own paper that could be helpful. One is the *Wall Street Journal,* the eminent, authoritative, up-to-date, but very readable daily business newspaper. The other is the accessible, respectable, highly relevant *Value Line Survey,* published by Value Line, Inc., New York. It contains invaluable insights into the stock and bond markets.

General magazines such as *Newsweek, Time, Business Week* and *U.S. News & World Report* all have current articles on trends, money and the overall economy. Peruse a few of them, just to get a feel for how various ideas are presented.

Observe the message in Proverbs 21:5, "Steady plodding brings prosperity; hasty speculation brings poverty." Isn't your financial independence worth 15 minutes of your time each day?

Before you begin looking at the various financial opportunities at your disposal, it's important you feel comfortable within the financial world. You must be able to identify relevant information that comes your way and recognize the trends that affect the money game.

> Can't you hear the voice of wisdom? She is standing at the city gates and at every fork in the road, and at the door of every house. Listen to what she says: "I have important information for you. Everything I say is right and true. . . . My advice is wholesome and good . . . . My words are plain and clear to anyone with half a mind—if it is only open!" (Prov. 8:1-3,7-9).

The "Four I's" are the beginning of successful stewardship. But they are only part of a process. Trusting your intuitions, involving yourself with the marketplace, informing yourself on business news, and identifying investment trends all require commitment. Added to all that, patience and perseverance will yield the wisdom you need to have financial savvy.

CHAPTER THREE
It's in the Numbers

Financial savvy is not only compatible with faith, but it also can be an integral part of faith. Further, as a woman, you have a right and a responsibility to gain and use this savvy. But where do you start?

The obvious answer is: at the beginning. Proverbs 27:23,24 counsels, "Riches can disappear fast. And the king's crown doesn't stay in his family forever—so watch your business interests closely. Know the state of your flocks and your herds." In other words, before you can take action, you must take stock. You need to know what your assets are, what tools you have to work with.

WHERE TO BEGIN:
DETERMINING YOUR NET WORTH

First, you need to determine your net worth. Net worth is found by calculating all of your assets, subtracting all of your debits or liabilities and looking at the final figure.

Whether you are single and head of household, or married and part of a larger family, you need to know how much you have to begin with.

Single women will have an easier time in determining their net worth because all assets are theirs exclusively. Married women have an additional initial decision to make: whether to determine net worth as a family or as an individual. A married woman is part of a unit, and thus may have a harder time determining what assets—as well as what liabilities!—are hers, what assets are his and what assets are joint.

For the sake of simplicity, most net worth statements can be calculated for the family, for all assets acquired and income earned during a marriage are considered jointly owned. Unless you hold significant separate assets, it is not only acceptable, but realistic to calculate net worth as a family. But in doing so, remember to discover how specifically each asset is listed and legally held.

Whether you consider net worth as a family or as an individual, it is important, indeed essential, to know exactly what's in your name, what's in his name and what is joint named—and that you agree. Even if all assets are considered joint property, how these assets are legally held may have significant implications. You should know in detail how your home is listed, how insurance policies are set up, how savings accounts are listed, in whose name the cars are owned, what mortgages or loans have your name on them, which credit cards are in his name or your name or joint names—and the list goes on.

Separate Property: What Is It?

If you have assets acquired prior to marriage, or if you

were gifted or inherited assets during marriage, these are your separate property and should be kept separate. If your Great-uncle Waldo gives you 200 shares of IBM and you decide to sell that stock in order to purchase others, the new stocks are still your separate property. Whatever the circumstances, you should have a clear understanding of the ownership of all your assets and of the responsibility for all your liabilities.

Your Personal Assessment

Let me introduce you to a form that will help you identify your assets and your liabilities. Remember, the final line, assets minus liabilities, will show your net worth. A good idea would be to add spaces to the right for the next two years, so that one day you can look back and see how your situation changed. (See next page.)

Now let's take a look at these areas one-by-one.

Checking In. I like to start with *checking accounts.* One of the reasons for going through the process step-by-step is to expose the deficiencies, the soft spots, in your current situation. And the one place where I find a surprising amount of poorly used money is in the non-interest bearing checking account. It never ceases to amaze me how much money is left sitting in these accounts.

In the 1970s through the mid-1980s, I ran an active financial planning firm. The number of new clients who came in with just a few dollars in their checking accounts was far exceeded by the number who had a great deal in theirs. Most never tuned into the simple fact that they could be earning interest on these monies on a day-to-day basis.

NET WORTH STATEMENT

Assets

1. Checking Accounts

   Bank: _____ Amount _____

   Bank: _____ Amount _____
   (should only contain one month's expenses)

   _____

2. Savings Accounts—Passbook

   Savings and Loan _____ Amount _____

   Savings and Loan _____ Amount _____

   Savings and Loan _____ Amount _____

   _____

3. Certificates of Deposit

	Rate	Matures	Amount
Bank or Savings and Loan _____	____	____	_____
Bank or Savings and Loan _____	____	____	_____
Bank or Savings and Loan _____	____	____	_____
Bank or Savings and Loan _____	____	____	_____

   _____

4. Money Market Funds

   Company _____ Amount _____

   Company _____ Amount _____

   _____

5. Credit Union _____ Amount _____

   Credit Union _____ Amount _____

   _____

6. Government Obligations

	Rate	Matures	Amount
Treasury Bills	____	____	_____
Treasury Bonds	____	____	_____
Treasury Notes	____	____	_____
Savings Bonds	____	____	_____

   _____

7. Bonds—Municipal and Corporate

Company or Municipality	Number of Bonds	Rate	Maturity	Original Cost	Market Value
_____	_____	_____	_____	_____	_____
_____	_____	_____	_____	_____	_____
_____	_____	_____	_____	_____	_____
_____	_____	_____	_____	_____	_____

_____

8. Retirement Accounts

IRAs   Amount _____

                                             Amount _____

Keoghs   Amount _____

401k Programs   Amount _____

                                             Amount _____

Other Employee Related Programs   Amount _____

_____

9. Annuities

	Rate	Amount
Company _____	_____	_____
Company _____	_____	_____

_____

10. Life Insurance—Cash Value

Company	Amount of Insurance	Cash Value
_____	_____	_____
_____	_____	_____

_____

11. Notes Due You from Others (Include Real Estate Trust Deeds)

Name	Amount	Rate	Matures	Value
_____	_____	_____	_____	_____
_____	_____	_____	_____	_____

_____

12. Stocks and Stock Options

Number of Shares	Company	Purchase Date	Original Cost	Dividends	Market Value
_____	_____	_____	_____	_____	_____
_____	_____	_____	_____	_____	_____
_____	_____	_____	_____	_____	_____
_____	_____	_____	_____	_____	_____
_____	_____	_____	_____	_____	_____

_____

13. Stock—Privately Held Companies—Nonliquid

Number of Shares	Company	Purchase Date	Original Cost	Dividends	Market Value
_____	_____	_____	_____	_____	_____
_____	_____	_____	_____	_____	_____
					_____

14. Mutual Funds

Number of Shares	Company	Purchase Date	Original Cost	Current Market
_____	_____	_____	_____	_____
_____	_____	_____	_____	_____
_____	_____	_____	_____	_____
				_____

15. Real Estate

	Location	Value
Residence	_____	_____
Second or Vacation Home	_____	_____
Income Property		
Apartments	_____	_____
Commercial Buildings	_____	_____
Other	_____	_____
		_____

16. Limited Partnerships

Company _____ Investment Amount _____
Company _____ Investment Amount _____
Company _____ Investment Amount _____

_____

17. Commodities

Individual Contracts _____
Managed Accounts _____

_____

18. Art _____
19. Jewelry and Furs _____
20. Coins _____
21. Antiques _____
22. Other Collectibles _____

_____

23. Personal Items

    Automobiles   _____

    Furniture   _____

    Other   _____

    _____

24. Other Assets   _____

    Total Assets   _____

———————————————— Liabilities ————————————————

1. Mortgages
    Residential   _____
    Second or Vacation   _____
    Income Property   _____   _____
2. Commercial Loans
    Automobile   _____
    Unsecured   _____
    Secured   _____   _____
3. Personal Debts
    IOU's   _____
    MasterCard   _____
    Visa   _____
    Other Credit Cards   _____
    Unpaid Taxes   _____
    Tithing Commitment   _____
    Dues & Loans   _____
    Other Obligations   _____
    _____
    _____   _____

    Total Liabilities   _____

    Net Worth (Total Assets minus Total Liabilities)   _____

In today's age of technology and electronic transfers, it only takes a few minutes over the phone to transfer funds into your account from savings or money market accounts to cover the checks you have just written, or are in the process of writing. That's, of course, assuming there is money in those accounts to take care of that need.

Rarely are men the culprits in leaving funds in non-interest bearing accounts. My experience has shown that if there is cash lying around, 95 percent of the time it will

---

I'm an advocate of keeping just enough funds in your checking account to cover your ongoing or current month's expenses.

---

be a woman who is steward of those funds.

Having money sitting around not doing anything is a problem that most of us would gladly entertain. There is, though, no sense in throwing good money away. This includes money not earning any interest, even for a day.

Savings Accounts—Passbook. With the declining interest rates 1986 brought about, some banks and savings and loans actually lowered their passbook rates from their 5-1/4 percent and 5-1/2 percent floors. Some dropped as low as 4-1/2 percent. Now, this doesn't sound too exciting, especially for those of you who remember when it was quite easy to get 17 percent on your cash via the money market funds in 1981.

Well, times have changed and they will continue to change. At some point, interest rates will go up again; at others, they will begin to decline. Your responsibility is to monitor those changes—the rise and the fall—and be savvy enough to move your funds around to receive the bare minimum of the best current interest rates available. I'm an advocate of keeping just enough funds in your checking account to cover your ongoing or current month's expenses. The rest of your monies should be actively working for you.

Some of you may receive a gift of a few hundred dollars, or thousands of dollars, from an inheritance, proceeds from a life insurance policy or a gain on an investment. The check arrives. Before you really have the opportunity to figure out what to do with it, you may just deposit the proceeds into your checking account. Your intentions are the best. Unfortunately, time has a habit of slipping by, often too quickly. One day grows to a few days, to weeks, sometimes even months before you become conscious that your overall return at this point is zero. When you do make a financial move, it may be too quickly and into the wrong situation.

The other side of that coin is that many times lump sums have a habit of being eroded. A little bit here, a little bit there—all dribbling away to a variety of worthwhile causes and needs—and then it's gone, or at least the bulk of it is.

Financial institutions are ecstatic when someone like I have just described opens up an account or adds to their already existing account. After all, this is how they make their money. They loan it out to others at a much higher rate than they would ever promise to give you on a simple passbook account.

Certificates of Deposit. Savings accounts, certificates of deposit and credit unions all have something in common. You, as the depositor, have agreed to place your funds with these institutions for a specific period of time—passbook savings account for one day; certificates of deposit can spawn for as many as 10 years. Credit unions offer day-to-day accounts, quarterly accounts and multi-year accounts.

Ideally, it makes sense to have approximately six months after-tax earnings placed in a combination of these accounts, or in liquid accounts. Liquidity is defined as anything that you can get your hands on within seven days.

When you place your funds with these groups, you are in effect making a loan. The bank agrees to give you a certain percent and you agree to leave your funds there for a specific period of time. The bank, savings and loan or credit union then proceeds to loan out your funds at a much higher rate. It can be anywhere from two to three times what you are currently receiving. This is how they make the bulk of their profit.

Money Market Funds. Money markets were birthed in the early '70s. Then, few people used them. In the late '70s, I would ask students in the classes I taught if they were familiar with money market funds. I felt lucky to get a 50 percent positive response. The 1980s changed that. With the high interest rates of '82, more than 80 percent of the students (average age of 40-plus) were aware of the term, and most had activated an account with them.

A money market fund is simply a mutual fund. It is a portfolio of money market instruments—treasury bills, bonds, notes, commercial paper, bankers acceptances, certificates of deposits. With the pooling of funds from people like you and me, amounting to many millions of dollars on a daily basis, they are able to participate in very large investments. Due to the volume of money market instruments they purchase, they often get a higher interest rate—a rate that you and I don't enjoy with our smaller funds. Having access to a money market fund is good financial sense.

Government Obligations. Assets that are designated as government obligations, as well as corporate and municipal bonds, all have something in common—you. You are loaning monies to Uncle Sam, the state or a corporation of your choice. In return, they will pay you interest twice a year and promise to give back your money anywhere from three months, as in the case of treasury bills, to 30-plus years, as in the case of the other bonds. Any interest received from investments in U.S. treasuries is tax-exempt on your state taxes, but taxable on your federal return.

Retirement Accounts. Every little bit you can put away in a retirement program should be done. Those little bits add up to a significant amount of money. In my book, *Money Phases: The Six Financial Stages of a Woman's Life,*[1] I stated that if a woman were able to save $2,000 a year in an IRA (Individual Retirement Account) beginning at the age of 18, and earned 12 percent per year, she would have invested a total of $94,000 by the time she was 65 (a 47-year period). That $94,000 at 12 percent compounded on a tax-deferred basis would have grown to $3,821,179.60—certainly a respectable amount of money and more than you will ever receive from Social Security.

I advise everyone to do an IRA, even if you can't take a deduction on your taxes. If you're self-employed, you can also contribute to a Keogh plan. IRAs have limitations of $2,000 per year contribution; Keogh, $30,000 per year.

A 401(k) is a special program set up by an employer for the benefit of the employee. A choice is usually offered as to where to put your money—in money market related accounts, fixed income accounts or in mutual fund growth accounts. You can contribute in excess of $7,000 per year; your employer can contribute funds in excess of that amount. Your W-2 at the end of the year excludes your contributions for a 401(k) program for federal and state tax purposes and taxes are deferred until you choose to withdraw the funds. Try to participate in any or all of the programs—IRA, Keogh, 401(k) and annuities—that allow for tax deferral.

Annuities. If you are conservative and want to minimize risk, annuities come into play. They are a life insurance product. Any tax due on growth or earnings is deferred until you actually withdraw funds at a later date.

When you buy an annuity, you purchase a contract that has specific terms—the amount of money involved, promised interest rate, length of time involved.

As you fill out your net worth statement all terms should be known. Annuities will be covered in depth in a later chapter.

Life Insurance. If you have a life insurance policy with a loan or cash value, dated prior to 1980, odds are you are getting a very low return on your money—2-½ to 3 percent. Do yourself a favor and review these policies at least every three years. The life insurance industry is in an ongoing revolution/evolution. It comes up with new products annually. The newer ones, such as the combination of an insurance policy and annuity, may be ideal if you find yourself straddling the fence or feeling conservative with your money and yet wanting it to grow at a faster rate than inflation.

When you let the funds build up in the form of cash values with an insurance policy, you are in actuality helping them to build those incredibly tall buildings on every corner of every major city. The insurance company invests your premium dollars in major real estate ventures with their name alone on them, not yours. Shop and compare. One policy will be quite similar to another company, but with a different name. The other difference is that the premium cost is greater or less, but rarely the same.

Notes Due You. Anyone who owes you money should state it in the form of a formal note. Loaning money out is business. If the person to whom you loan funds is unable to pay you back, you can then declare it as a loss on your tax return. A word of advice here: I highly recommend when you make loans to friends or family, you mentally think of the loans as gifts. If you get them back, great. But if you don't, is it really worth terminating or severely damaging a relationship? Loaned money causes more problems in families and friendships than almost any other single item I can think of.

Real Estate Trust Deeds. If you sold a piece of property and needed to carry back paper or a note to make the deal work, it should have been done in the form of a recorded trust deed. This means that if the person who bought your property sells or refinances it, you are recorded as holding a lien against the property. The sale or refinancing can't be completed until you OK it—either by subordinating your note to someone else's note or demanding pay-off at the close of the new sale or refinancing.

Make sure the note you carry back is recorded in the county in which the property is located. The title company will pick up the outstanding obligation when a preliminary title search is done when escrow is opened for the future sale. If the note is not recorded, you may be stuck in pursuing the borrower for your funds.

If you're in the middle of selling a piece of real estate and a note is being considered, make sure you check out the ongoing rates for private financing. You can usually get a little bit higher rate than what a commercial bank will offer and your loan will normally be for a shorter period of time, such as three to five years. I also recommend getting a credit report on the prospective borrowers. Remember, you are now acting as a bank, which wouldn't loan money without considering a credit check or employment verification. Why should you?

Stocks and Stock Options. This brings us to a section on the balance sheet I like to identify as working dollars. Stocks, mutual funds and real estate are primary components of this area. Although no stock is valued at more than what it can be sold for on any particular day, it is still important to know what the ongoing market value is. It is also essential to know when the stock was purchased and its original cost.

Mutual Funds. The stock market action of the 1980s has brought a great deal of attention to mutual funds. For the small investor, a woman who has less than $10,000 to invest, mutual funds become an attractive alternative to just buying shares of stock.

There are a variety of funds to choose from. If you purchased shares and receive a share certificate that represents your total investment, look up the fund in the quotation section of your newspaper. Then, multiply your total shares by the "bid" price that's reported.

If the mutual fund holds your shares for you, as a rule, they report the total value on the monthly statements that are mailed directly to you.

In either case, the total amount is reported on your net worth statement.

Real Estate. One of the biggest assets you are likely to have is your home. Pre-1960 homes appreciated minimally in value. It was a toss-up whether to buy or rent. Today it's different. With the humongous inflation of the 1970s, homes purchased initially for $20,000 or $30,000 saw their values increase many times over. These same houses today could be selling anywhere from $100,000 to $250,000, depending upon where in the country you live. One of our church members retired to the coast of central California with her husband. In building their dream home, Doris remarked the cabinets alone cost more than their first home. Do you know the original cost of your home? You should, and you should have an estimation of its current market value, as well.

Equity in a home or in any piece of real estate is determined by deducting the loan balance from the current market value. This could be a windfall for you in later years. It could supply the necessary funds for education, unusual medical expenses, even relocating to a different area where the cost of living is higher than the one in which you are currently living.

If you own any other real estate, such as a vacation home, raw land, even a condominium that you have a time-share interest in, include these on your net worth statement. It makes sense to keep an updated estimation on the market value. Don't assume the real estate assessor's valuation of your property is valid. More than likely, it will be considerably below what yours could sell for in the open market.

If you are unclear in this area of real estate, scout around and see if any houses or similar properties in your immediate area have sold within the last few months. If they have, you'll be able to get a fair estimation of what yours might be worth. Or, contact one of the many brokers and tell them you're interested in determining the value of your house; although you are not currently moving, you may be sometime in the future. Real estate is a service business, so most agents will be happy to assist you. I would, however, suggest you discount their appraisal by a few thousand dollars. Often, they come in somewhat high in an attempt to entice you to list with them.

Limited Partnerships. When investors *pool* their funds to purchase an investment, like an apartment(s) or a commercial building(s), they may do it in a legal entity such as a limited partnership. Limited partnerships are difficult to value. If it's a public partnership—one in which there are over 35 partners—you might simply list the original amount you invested. That is, unless you know it has declined significantly in value and/or it has had sales that will produce a greater return at a future time when funds are disbursed.

If it's a private partnership—under 35 investors—the person who is general partner (manager) may be able to assist you in a determination. I have been in limited partnerships in which all the investors made a handsome return and I've been in other partnerships where we've lost everything. Always keep in mind there are no guarantees.

Commodities. Unless you are a farmer or have substantial monies, avoid commodities. Period.

Collectibles. No net worth statement would be complete without taking into consideration personal assets and collectibles. These include art, diamonds, stamp collections, coins, jewelry, furs—anything of intrinsic value. Since values oscillate every few years, it would be wise to have a re-appraisal done not only for insurance purposes, but for your own personal knowledge. Once you pay for an appraisal, all that's usually necessary on a re-appraisal is to take in the old appraisal to the original appraising firm, who can then adjust their evaluations based on the current market place.

Personal property is an area that most of us tend to undervalue. But think for a moment. Imagine someone coming up to your front door with a giant vacuum, flicking the switch, and watching everything disappear—your wall hangings, your furniture, clothes, kitchen dishes and appliances, stereo, all your personal items. It would cost a lot of money to replace these items. Guesstimate as to what all these items would cost to replace.

Other Assets. Many of you, for a variety of reasons, have minimal assets. In fact, some of you have a negative net worth—you owe more than you actually have. Generally speaking, your liabilities should be less than your assets. The difference is your net worth. If your liabilities actually exceed your assets, you have a negative net worth. You may be just starting out with a few charge accounts but no real hard assets to your name; or you may have spent the last few years studying at an educational institution for your career, or you may have just given up your job to marry or have a baby and you find yourself overextended. It seems you have nothing but debt. All is not lost. There's

---

Seeing where your money goes is more than half the effort required to be able to budget where it should go.

---

one more item on a net worth statement, and that's for you. Other assets. Put your name down and put in a dollar amount of what you feel you are really worth.

Your best asset is yourself. Your ability to work hard and long toward an objective and the motivation to achieve the objective will probably outweigh any temporary negative net worth. The important thing is to know where you stand right now.

Knowing where you stood a year ago or where you might stand a year from now is important in the financial planning process. Regular updates of your net worth can be revealing measures of your financial progress, of your success or failures in meeting goals. If you have the information, try to calculate your net worth as of a year ago. The comparison will tell you an even fuller story about your financial situation.

EVALUATING YOUR CASH FLOW

In addition to net worth, you must also evaluate your cash flow. This is something like a budget in reverse. Instead of planning where your dollars should go, you chart exactly where they went. Only then can you get an overview of your spending. Adjustments can then be made to cut down on frills, keep up with the necessary expenditures without going into debt, and put money aside for investments.

On the following page is a monthly chart that can help you evaluate your cash flow. Seeing where your money goes is more than half the effort required to be able to budget where it *should* go. This type of cash flow chart will enable you to make preparations for those months when you have bigger than usual expenditures—hence the need for more cash on hand. At year's end, you will have a valuable tool in reviewing how your financial plan is progressing.

Looking at the hard numbers is your initiation to the world of money—the groundwork to let you begin to take control. Proverbs 24:3,4 says it succinctly: "Any enterprise is built by wise planning, becomes strong through common sense, and profits wonderfully by keeping abreast of the facts."

No one enjoys compiling net worth statements or tracking every detail of everyday expenditures. But this is the kind of information you need to be able to make the most of what you've got. It's the information you need to be able to emulate the ants talked about in Proverbs 6:6-11:

> Take a lesson from the ants, you lazy fellow. Learn from their ways and be wise! For though they have no king to make them work, yet they labor hard all summer, gathering food for the winter. But you—all you do is sleep. When will you wake up? "Let me sleep a little longer!"

DEVELOPING A PLAN

	BUDGETED	ACTUAL
INCOMING:		
Alimony/Child Support	_____	_____
Bonuses	_____	_____
Capital Gains (the increase in value of an asset over purchase price at the time you sell it)	_____	_____
Commissions	_____	_____
Dividends	_____	_____
Gifts	_____	_____
Interest	_____	_____
Other Income	_____	_____
Rental Property	_____	_____
Retirement, Pensions	_____	_____
Salary	_____	_____
TOTAL CASH IN	_____	_____

	BUDGETED	ACTUAL
OUTGOING:		
Child Care	_____	_____
Clothing	_____	_____
Contributions	_____	_____
Credit Card Payments	_____	_____
Dues	_____	_____
Education (books, tuition, seminars)	_____	_____
Entertainment	_____	_____
Gasoline	_____	_____
Gifts	_____	_____
Groceries	_____	_____
Home Furnishings	_____	_____
Household Supplies	_____	_____
Installment Payments	_____	_____
Insurance	_____	_____
Life	_____	_____
Automobile	_____	_____

Homeowners		
Medical		
Other		
Investments		
Loan Payments		
Medical and Dental		
Medicine, Drugs		
Mortgage Payments or Rent		
Personal Care		
Repairs		
Auto		
Appliances		
Home		
Other		
Savings		
Subscriptions		
Taxes		
Federal (withheld)		
Federal (quarterly)		
State (withheld)		
State (quarterly)		
FICA (Social Security)		
State Disability Insurance		
General Sales		
County or City		
Tithing		
Transportation		
Utilities, Gas or Oil		
Electric		
Garbage		
Telephone		
Vacation		
Other		

TOTAL CASH OUT (Difference between cash in, cash out) _____

Sure, just a little more! And as you sleep, poverty creeps upon you like a robber and destroys you; want attacks you in full armor.

Note
1. Judith Briles, *Money Phases: The Six Financial Stages of a Woman's Life* (New York: Simon and Schuster, 1984).

CHAPTER FOUR

Tithing, Of Course!

When it comes to tithing, most Christians shuffle the word into their back closet. Other terms, *pledging,* or even better, *giving,* emerge. It was Voltaire who said, "When it is a question of money, everybody is of the same religion." Unfortunately, his statement is vindicated far too often. The old joke, where during an emergency a pastor is asked to "do something religious," so he takes up a collection, is cause enough for many people to stay away from church altogether.

Over a three-year period, I served as stewardship chair for my church. A few of our members tithed through their pledges, with some even pledging well in excess of 10 percent of their gross income. But the great majority gave a fraction of what they could, and did so haphazardly. Crumpled or folded one-dollar bills filled the Sunday offering plate.

Many times I wished each member could be the Sunday money counter, unwadding all those single bills and still finding a total that nowhere met the need. It was not an issue of whether the members had the funds—many spent enormous sums on trips, trinkets or other material items. Their giving was coming out of leftovers, *after* the new car, private schools, summer camps, trips and clothes were paid for. Our members were *unconscious* of the call of tithing; unconscious of the real needs of the church; unconscious of their own ability, not to mention opportunity, to give.

Tithing does not have to be such a reprehensible concept. It does not deserve to be tainted with such hostility. I think too many of us see tithing as a burdensome obligation, a law we don't like. In fact, the principle of tithing is set forth early in the Bible. In Genesis, Abraham gave tithes to Melchizedek, "a priest of the God of Highest Heaven," (Gen. 14:18): "Then Abram gave Melchizedek a tenth of all the spoils." (v.20).

Throughout the Old and New Testaments, giving, sharing, even tithing, are presented as opportunities. I believe that tithing is a key ingredient to our development as Christians. It doesn't come naturally; it may need to be learned. But sooner or later, we all need to face up to the responsibility of our Christian stewardship of money.

> On every Lord's Day each of you should put aside something from what you have earned during the week, and use it for this offering. The amount depends on how much the Lord has helped you earn. Don't wait until I get there and then try to collect it all at once (1 Cor. 16:2).
>
> But remember this—if you give little, you will get little. A farmer who plants just a few seeds will get only a small crop, but if he plants

much, he will reap much. Every one must make up his own mind as to how much he should give. Don't force anyone to give more than he really wants to, for cheerful givers are the ones God prizes (2 Cor. 9:6,7).

A SOLUTION—NOT A PROBLEM

I'd like to show you how tithing can be a solution, not a problem. It can be a solution for you, spiritually, as a Christian; for you as a member and supporter of your church, which is an on-going operational entity; and even for you as financial steward and money manager.

To tithe is to trust. It is to acknowledge that God will provide, that God will protect.

Let's start with you as a Christian. Remember the back closet, the one we often shuffle the word *tithe* into? If you shuffle too many obligations into it, it becomes a Fibber McGee closet, the kind where all sorts of odds and ends start to fall out if you even crack the door. At first you simply slam the door shut to keep everything inside. Soon you don't even open the door at all. When you stop opening that door, the door hiding your uncomfortable, maybe scary obligations, you begin to forget a cornerstone of Christian reality—the reality that you may possess, but ultimately, God owns. "Bring this tithe to eat before the Lord your God at the place he shall choose as his sanctuary; this applies to your tithes of grain, new wine, olive oil, and the firstborn of your flocks and herds.

The purpose of tithing is to teach you always to put God first in your lives." (Deut. 14:23).

To tithe is to trust. It is to acknowledge that God will provide, that God will protect. "Trust in your money and down you go! Trust in God and flourish as a tree!" (Prov. 11:28).

NO MORE LEFTOVERS

Another spiritual benefit inherent in tithing is that you are no longer giving leftovers. You are *starting* with your commitment to God, not ending with it. In my years as a financial advisor, I was always amazed when my clients told me they didn't know where their money went—they just didn't have enough. One remedy was to get out their checkbook and start tracking. I knew a disaster was lurking when they told me they had a cash withdrawal card from their bank or savings and loan. These cards are trouble, with a capital *T* for just about everyone. When you have cash, it easily disappears. Instead of withdrawing $20, you decide to take $40, $60 even $100! And then it mysteriously dwindles—movies, incidentals, snacks, often nonsense items. Your money literally vanishes overnight.

SO MANY EXCUSES

It was the same for many members in my church. I would query them if I hadn't had a response during our pledging time or if the amount promised was very low. Could or would they make a greater commitment? Responses were varied, but connected. They had other obligations—those trips, trinkets, new cars, camps and lessons for the kids. There just wasn't much left over to give to the church. There it was again: leftover. Most had those cash withdrawal cards—where were the 10 and 20-dollar bills that had slid out from those machines? Certainly not in the collection plate. We got the one-dollar bills and sometimes a rare five—the leftovers.

I wish the teller machines could be banned, but they won't be. So it falls on you to take control. Money is a gift from God—not from the automatic teller machine!

With a sigh of relief, I began my last year as stewardship chair. I tried to think of something that might motivate our congregation to commit to giving at the beginning of the pledge drive. In the past I had told amusing stories, read from Scripture, even dressed myself as a Christmas tree and asked for their support. One day, I found myself in Matthew, chapter seven. How interesting. Matthew was a tax collector and a passage from him is appropriate indeed. "Ask, and you will be given what you ask for. Seek, and you will find. Knock, and the door will be opened. For everyone who asks, receives. Anyone who seeks, finds. If only you will knock, the door will open" (Matt. 7:7,8).

I asked, I knocked . . . one more time. Pledging *finally* began to increase from our members, setting the stage for the new stewardship chair.

A NEED FILLED

Tithing also offers a solution for the needs of your church. The church has a Fibber McGee closet as well, only it's odds-and-ends expenses that fill it up. When the church cracks the door of its closet, needs and wants fall out, needs and wants that can only be fulfilled if church members decide to open their closets as well.

Churches are regular operating institutions. They struggle to take care of maintenance, ongoing staff and salary expenses and regular operating needs such as utilities and insurance. Too often, church improvements are out of the question, and monies that are optimistically allocated in the year's budget for missions never find their way.

You may be surprised to learn there is a financial blessing in tithing, which fits into any sound financial planning.

Just as you are working to be financially free in order to devote time and energy to other aspects of life, so the church would be financially free if every Christian would tithe 10 percent of his or her income. What exists instead is paralysis. Because most churches don't have members who tithe, their ongoing status is in a continual state of flux. "Bring all the tithes into the storehouse so that there will be food enough in my Temple; if you do, I will open up the windows of heaven for you and pour out a blessing so great you won't have room enough to take it in! (Mal. 3:10).

GIVE—AND YOU SHALL RECEIVE

Blessings can come in many ways. You may be surprised to learn there is a financial blessing in tithing, which fits into any sound financial planning. First of all, for many Christians, tithing frees them to feel good and open about savvy stewardship of their monies. Tithing establishes a foundation and a priority. It also reminds us that money is a gift from God—not from the automatic teller machine!

Furthermore, tithing is an excellent income tax deduction. Ten percent from the top of the gross income is a small sum to pay when compared with the 20 to 30 percent-plus the federal and state governments extract from most paychecks.

ACTIONS SPEAK: ARE YOU LISTENING?

In the end, tithing works. It's a critical element in successful Christian money management. Isn't it time you opened the door and made a commitment? Will you move your giving to tithing by making it a priority in your life, by consciously sharing from your gross income and not give leftovers?

When you tithe, you do it for yourself and God, not for someone else. Every woman and man I have met who tithes is quite bold in his/her common statement, "The more I give, the more I get."

As a faithful person in Christ, isn't it time for you to get more . . . by giving more?

CHAPTER FIVE

Taxes: Lightening the Load

When it comes to taxes, it is easy to say that the one thing you can be assured of is they will change—up, down, even sideways. As an author, I am always concerned about being dated with the material I present to my reader. Knowing that what is OK today may be totally different tomorrow makes my head swim, as it probably does yours. Congress and the taxing authorities are almost crazed in their swings from year to year. Tax-law experts—both lawyers and accountants—shake their heads at what "they" in Washington, D.C., come up with. It seems like a never-ending cycle.

This ever-changing tax environment demands that you take the responsibility to keep up with areas that will have a direct impact on you and your family. *The tax information presented in this chapter is subject to change. I strongly advise you to check with your financial consultant, accountant or tax lawyer to verify what is current and if a suggested strategy or deduction is still allowable before you begin an action plan.*

To many, taxes are simply another form of tithing—a necessary, exacted payment based on annual earnings. After all, Caesar must get his due. "Obey the laws," the Bible says, "for two reasons: first, to keep from being punished, and second, just because you know you should. Pay your taxes too, for these same two reasons" (Rom. 13:5,6).

Income taxes, of course, must be paid. But there are some important differences between tithing and taxing. First, the payee is different. You give to the church from choice; it is a value judgment; an extension of your faith, and you trust the church will use your money wisely. "If you want favor with both God and man, and a reputation for good judgment and common sense, then trust the Lord completely" (Prov. 3:4,5).

If you give to the government on demand, you have no direct control over your money's use; tax monies have little to do with morality, compassion or faith. There is one other important difference—the church asks for a straight donation; the government provides numerous legal sanctions, even encourages methods to *reduce your tax debt.*

There is no question that most people could pay far less income tax than they do and still remain in the good graces of the Internal Revenue Service. Much of your early effort in executing a financial strategy will be aimed at whittling down, by legal means, the amount of your taxable income. Tax planners and lawmakers have decided that certain tax exemptions and incentives will serve to stimulate the economy to benefit the family and to serve the capitalistic system.

The methods are there. It's up to you to use them to divert your monies from a seemingly bottomless hole, into creative investments, investments that will enrich your life and allow you to channel both energy and money into more meaningful endeavor. Taxes are a part of everyday life, but God and Caesar need not be exclusive. "What a shame—yes, how stupid!—to decide before knowing the facts!" (Prov. 18:13).

What then are some of these facts that can reduce your tax payments? One of the biggest and most prevalent problems in the decade of the '80s was tax reform. In the ten years from 1980 to 1990, there were six major changes in the tax laws, which at times totally eliminated areas that were legitimate and accepted as qualified deductions. It is imperative to keep abreast of these changes, perhaps through a financial planner, but certainly from your own readings.

One place to start is with your itemized deductions. An appalling majority of my clients have come to me failing to have claimed all deductions due them. If you're serious about a financial plan, you need to become familiar with what can be deducted and how to substantiate the deductions.

RECORD KEEPING IS VITAL

If you are going to use the tax laws to your advantage, you must keep accurate records of your financial transactions. Some of my clients are meticulous about tracking every dollar they spend. An enormous amount of time is spent on record keeping and detailing expenses so that when tax time comes around, they merely total up the bottom lines. However, there is no correct way to do this.

I confess I'm a stockpiler. I simply accumulate all tax-related data during the year (receipts, bank records, cancelled checks, stock and interest information, etc.) in one

place—a folder or drawer designated for that purpose—
and then spend two days each year dividing, organizing
and totaling. Whichever method you use, be religious
about it. If you question a receipt or expense, keep or
record it anyway. An accountant can advise you, but only if
the information is there to work with.

A useful tool for record keeping is a detailed, accurate
desk journal or calendar. It's a central place to record mileage driven for business purposes, including your destina-
tion and purpose for the trip, business-related meals and
expenses, including who you met and why, child care and
medical expenses, cash donations and other related areas.
There's an old saying in real estate: To be successful, you
must buy location, location, location. To be successful in
the area of record keeping for the tax game, especially if
an audit comes your way: Think documentation, documentation, documentation.

TAX RATES

In the preceding chapter, I shared Matthew 7:7,8: "Ask,
and you will be given what you ask for. Seek, and you will
find. Knock, and the door will be opened. For everyone
who asks, receives. Anyone who seeks, finds. If only you
will knock, the door will open."

Somehow I think the Internal Revenue Service took
this and ran with it. They are knocking, seeking and looking for doors to be opened by every taxpayer and potential
taxpayer.

Matthew's words are straightforward and simple. The
IRS is under the illusion, and it is an illusion, that their
rules and laws are straightforward and simple. Aha, you
think, they are anything but!

The different tax bracket categories were reduced by the 1986 Tax Reform Act; there are fewer categories relating to income ranges. Unfortunately, the IRS is on a continual quest. I suspect the rates listed below will change again as the IRS tries to open more doors.

Any strategy you implement or consider implementing

Tax Rate Tables
(Taxable Years Beginning in 1990)

Unmarried

Taxable Income		Pay +	Tax Rate
Over	Not Over		
$ 0	$ 17,850	$ 0	15%
17,850	43,150	2,678	28%
43,150	100,480*	9,762	33%
100,480	or over	28,680	28%

Head of Household

$ 0	$ 23,900	$ 0	15%
23,900	61,650	3,585	28%
61,650	145,630*	14,155	33%
145,630	or over	41,868	28%

Married Filing Joint Return
(and qualifying Widows and Widowers)

$ 0	$ 29,750	$ 0	15%
29,750	71,900	4,463	28%
71,900	171,090*	16,265	33%
171,090	or over	48,997	28%

*The 33% bracket includes a 5% subtax for the phase-out of the benefits of the 15% tax bracket. The 33% tax bracket is extended by an additional $11,480 for each personal exemption.

will tie into your tax rate at some time or another. If you buy a house with a mortgage, it reduces your taxable income; if you have a loss or gain on any investment, it adjusts your taxable income accordingly.

Therefore, you are going to need to get out your calculator, pencil and paper, and determine whether your income will increase, as in a gain, or be reduced. Any changes in overall tax liability should be reflected by an adjustment on your W-4 if you and/or your spouse are employed. A sample W-4 is at the end of this chapter with step-by-step how-to's for filling it out.

Remember, Uncle Sam does not pay interest on tax refunds and you may risk a penalty if you underwithhold on taxes.

Confused? Don't be. It's really not that hard to understand.

Let's suppose you are married and have one child. You work part time and earn $10,000. Your husband earns $36,500 per year. You have excess deductions of $8,125, a stock loss of $2,025 and no credits. You anticipate that your savings and stock dividends will total $2,000. Each personal exemption is worth $2,050 in 1990. Here is your roadmap:

Step 1.

Income	$46,500
Interest/dividends	2,000
Excess deductions	-8,125
Stock loss	-2,025
Personal exemptions (3x2,050)	-6,150
Taxable income	$32,200

In reviewing the married, filing jointly tables, your taxable income falls in the 28 percent tax bracket between $29,750 and $71,900. You now need to figure the excess amount of taxes over the base of $29,750 at 28 percent ($32,200-29,750=$2,450). Add it to the minimum tax of $4,463 and, Alas!, your total tax obligation.

Step 2.

Taxable income	$32,200
Base	-29,750
Overage	2,450
Tax Rate	× .28
Additional tax	$686

Step 3.

Minimum tax	$4,463
Overage	+ $686
Total Tax	$5,149

Continue to review your situation from this base— raises, new position, new investments, losses, gains, etc. Any amount over $500 should lead you to re-check your withholding and your W-4.

OTHER INCOME AND DEDUCTIONS

Let's examine some of the deductions currently allowed.

Charitable Deductions

There are two contributions sections on your itemized tax return. Part A is for contributions for which you have cancelled checks and Part B is for cash contributions or items donated to charitable causes. It is in the latter area I find most individuals substantially underestimating their donations. Clothing, for instance, can be conservatively claimed up to 25 percent of fair market value. These types of contributions are limited to 30 percent of your adjusted gross income (AGI).

The adjusted gross income is calculated by taking all your income sources and then adjusting for factors such as an IRA or Keogh contribution, deductions for rental properties, any pension distributions, any gains or losses, any distributions from a profit sharing fund—it's all the income and adjustments before the final deduction on your tax form for itemized deductions as well as personal exemptions.

In the past, it has been limited to 50 percent of your AGI. If you use cash to give to various organizations, including your church on Sunday mornings, try to change that habit. If you don't have accurate records from the issuing organization as to exactly how much you have given, then you'll find there are severe limitations if you get audited in this area. I have sat in on audits with clients where the maximum allowed for a cash contribution was $50 per year. A $5 to $10 cash contribution every week certainly exceeds $50. Why risk losing that deduction? Write a check instead.

In the case of checks, as well as gifts of stocks or bonds given as deductions to a qualified organization, such as your church, contributions are generally limited to 50 percent of your AGI. This doesn't mean you can't give more than 50 percent, but merely that you cannot take a deduction on your tax return for more than that amount.

Always keep in mind your time cannot be calculated as

having a value, although it is certainly recognized as valuable. You *will* be allowed to take a deduction of 12 cents per mile if you use your car in performing services for your church or other qualified charities.

Medical Expenses

Medical and dental expenses have also undergone changes in this latest tax reform bill. In the past, you could deduct amounts in excess of 5 percent of your AGI. Beginning in 1987, that number had been changed to 7-½ percent. Let's assume your AGI was $30,000 and your combined unreimbursed medical expenses were $3,000. Your calculation would be as follows: 7-½ percent of $30,000 is $2,250. You would then deduct $2,250 from $3,000, leaving you with an excess deduction of $750. Don't forget to keep track of mileage. The IRS allows medical expense deductions of 9¢ per mile.

Taxes

Certain types of taxes paid throughout the year are included as an itemized deduction. Deductions are allowed for state and local income taxes, as well as real estate taxes. You can no longer take an itemized deduction for general sales taxes. These would include taxes you paid at the store, on automobiles, furniture and other big-ticket items.

Interest

Deductible interest includes that paid on your home, as well as vacation property. In 1987, deductibility of consumer interest started phasing out. This includes car loans, student loans, insurance policy loans, credit cards and other personal loans. The year 1987 saw 65 percent of consumer interest as deductible, 40 percent in 1988, 20 percent in 1989, 10 percent in 1990, and no deductibility in 1991 and thereafter.

For the past few years, various members of Congress have proposed that the deductibility of home mortgage interest be excluded or dramatically reduced as in Canada where no mortgage interest deductions are allowed by Canadian taxpayers. As of today, interest limitations come into play at the million dollar level for United States taxpayers. But then, who has a million-dollar mortgage—certainly not mid-America! The odds are that the mortgage interest deduction will remain a "sacred cow"—it will be talked about, threatened, but in the end, remain.

Automobiles
Automobile-related expenses is another area that could be deductible. Any expense incurred to and from work is not deductible. However, if you need a vehicle to assist you during business for client calls, or to attend business functions, you may have a valid deduction. The key is to keep track.

First of all, you need to determine how much of the car usage is business-related. Keep track of your mileage for a few months and determine whether it is typical of your full year. If you find that 50 percent of your car usage is devoted to business, this becomes very worthwhile.

The IRS will allow a deduction of 26 cents per mile for all business miles driven. Or you can choose the alternative method of taking the expenses of operating and maintaining the car—gas, oil, depreciation—and deduct those. Again, the key is documentation. You need receipts, especially for anything over $25, which will be tossed out in an audit if you can't prove it.

All expenses in excess of 2 percent of the AGI can be

deducted in the itemized deductions section of your tax return.

Business Deductions—
Meals, Travel, Entertainment

Only 80 percent of meals and entertainment expenses are deductible. If you are someone who travels a great deal, you may be able to get 100 percent deductibility. How? By attending a conference or a convention where banquet meetings are included, more than 50 percent of the participants are away from home, at least 40 people attend and the conference includes a speaker.

In order to deduct any meals, they must be directly related or associated with your business, and they can't be lavish or extravagant, although the IRS does not share with us its definition of lavish or extravagant. To me, New York's Russian Tea Room is extravagant. The Velvet Turtle or Chart House restaurants in the West are not.

No deductions will be allowed for meals related to investment purposes, costs for attending conventions or seminars for non-business purposes, educational travel expenses or financial planning seminars.

Uniforms

If you are required to wear a uniform for your job, its cost is deductible, as well as its cleaning and upkeep. If you work in a field such as nursing, which would require you to wear a particular kind of watch, then any replacement or repair costs would also be deductible.

Alimony

If you are required to pay alimony, those funds will be deductible. If you are a recipient, it is taxable income to you. If, for whatever reason, you are separated or divorced yet reside in the same household as your ex-partner, any payments made cannot be deducted. Good news for you as the recipient—you don't have to declare the money as income if you file a separate tax return.

Moving Expenses

If you take a new job that requires you to relocate, you have legitimate moving expenses. In addition to the actual costs of moving your household goods, there are other acceptable expenses. These include the cost of moving you and other members of your family, meals and lodging en route, temporary living expenses for up to 30 days, expenses of traveling (including meals and hotels) between your former residence and the new location when searching for a new home after obtaining employment.

There are some limitations, however. The new location must be at least 35 miles from the previous place of employment. There are dollar limitations that exist depending upon types of expenses. Any reimbursement from your employer for moving expenses or relocation costs must be reported as income. Finally, any expenses incidental to the sale or purchase of a home—for example, attorneys' fees, commissions or settlement expenses—are deductible up to a maximum of $3,000.

These various costs are not subject to any minimum percentage of the AGI. As are medical mileage deductions, moving mileage is also deductible at 9¢ per mile.

Casualty and Theft Losses

Deductions of losses caused by a sudden, unexpected or unusual event include thefts, fire, storm, vandalism or accidents. Amounts deductible must exceed 10 percent of the AGI after a $100 adjustment or deductible is taken into consideration. Any monies or property that is misplaced or has been damaged from termites or insects is not deductible. There are special rules that permit the deductibility of losses for your current tax year but apply to the preceding year. This can be taken if the President of the United States declares your situation a disaster.

Business losses are different and can be used for planning purposes. The IRS will allow you to carry a loss back for three years and if not absorbed by your income during those years, it can then be carried forward up to 15 years. If you find yourself in a situation where you have losses that can be carried back, you may find that you will get a tax refund for those years.

Capital Gains and Losses
All gains are taxed at your highest tax bracket. But capital losses are different. If you have a loss and a gain, they will be netted against each other. Only $3,000 of a loss is deductible against your ordinary income. Any remaining amount must be carried forward and used up each year at the same rate until exhausted.

Passive Income and Losses
The IRS has expanded its interpretation of the word *passive,* and how it applies to you as an investor. The most recent tax acts greatly restricted using losses from some activities (such as real estate) to offset income from others.

Proverbs 10:4 warns, "Lazy men are soon poor; hard workers get rich." Good enough, and I agree. But it's important to define lazy, which many in Congress say is passive. The folks in Washington, D.C., decided that any losses, either on paper or real, which were created in a passive investment or activity, would have severe limitations as an offset against other income.

Before I go further with this profound concept, you need to divvy your income, or losses, into three categories. This first is business income and wages, the second is dividend and interest and the third includes *passive*—the ones you supposedly don't participate in materially.

The rules generated from the Tax Reform Act of 1986 stated that passive losses and credits can *only* offset passive income. So, what does materially participate really mean? Being a limited partner excludes you as an active participant; if you own rental property, perhaps even several pieces, you are considered passive. But, if you are a general partner in an oil and gas limited partnership or continually involved in a business in trade, you are now a producer of active income (see chapter 13 on Limited Partnerships).

If you have ever been involved in the management of real estate, rarely can it be considered passive. Pressure forced the IRS to allow a deduction of up to $25,000 in passive losses that are generated to rental real estate against any non-passive income, if your AGI is less than $100,000—that's the great majority of us. I wouldn't be surprised to see the ceiling lifted further on the $25,000 loss offset rule. What Washington needs to learn is that lazy and passive are not synonymous—fixing leaky roofs in the middle of a storm or responding to broken pipes, is not passive in an owner's view of real estate.

If you have a vacation or second home, ignore the above section. You have no limitation to the amount of real estate taxes and mortgage interest you can write off.

DEFERRED COMPENSATION AND
RETIREMENT PLANS

Any program that involves deferred compensation should be considered as long-range planning. If you work for a business that has either a profit sharing plan or a defined benefit plan, the current tax laws have a significant effect on you. The 1986 Tax Reform Act stated that all employees in a plan must be fully vested by the end of the fifth or seventh year, depending upon which schedule a company must meet. For example, if you work seven years for a company in existence before the 1986 act, and decide to leave, then you will take with you not only your full contribution, but any growth, as well as contributions made by the company. If that company comes into existence after the tax act, it is necessary to work there only five years to become fully vested. In the old days, most companies counted on employees changing their jobs, thus leaving their "retirement" behind. The beneficiaries, of course, were the older employees and the owners.

ESOPs

An *employee stock ownership plan* has similar benefits of profit sharing plans. In this particular plan, the corporate employer contributes shares of its own stock to the ESOP trust. No cash changes hands, but the corporation gets a tax deduction for the total value of the stock, and you, the employee, do not get taxed until you take the funds out at a later date. Many companies offer ESOP plans to their employees and welcome the side effects. They found that when employees actually own part of the stock of the issuing company, there is an increased incentive to perform well, which can lead to higher profits. The net results: a higher stock market value on the underlying stock.

Incentive Stock Options

Incentive stock options carry no tax consequence when the option is originally granted or exercised; exercised meaning that you as the employee actually paid for them and have them delivered to you or to a fiduciary entity such as a brokerage firm or a bank on your behalf. When an option is granted, it merely means it's held in place in your name, and at a specified later date you can buy them. Taxes are finally paid when the shares are sold, which, of course, will be at your choice.

401(k) Plans

Another form of deferred compensation or salary reduction plan is the 401(k). These plans enjoyed a great deal of popularity in the mid-1980s and must be sponsored by an employer who can, at his or her option, contribute to the plan on your behalf. You, as the employee, agree in writing to have your salary reduced by a fixed percentage amount. Current law allows you to make a contribution in excess of $7,000 of your gross earnings. If you have a 401(k) program available to you, make every effort to participate. It is these deferral dollars that add up to so much at a later time. The maximum contribution will be adjusted each year by the IRS guidelines. Make sure you check any revisions with your tax advisor. This is one area in which you want to participate your monies to the maximum amount allowed.

IRAs

If you participate in a retirement program where you work, you can no longer deduct your entire contribution. A partial deduction is available if you are single and your AGI is less than $35,000; if you are married, less than

$50,000. No deduction will be available if your AGI exceeds these amounts. The partial deductibility begins to be taken into consideration if your AGI ranges from $25,000 to $35,000 as a single, and $40,000 to $50,000 if married. This means for every $1,000 in AGI over the $25,000 and $40,000 minimums, you lose $200 in deductibility.

You can, though, make a non-deductible contribution up to the maximum of $2,000. These funds will accumulate on a tax deferred basis until you withdraw them.

The spousal IRA of $250 is still available. As with the 401(k) programs, it is strongly recommended that contributions be made to an IRA even if non-deductible on your taxes. As of this writing, Congress is still considering "fine-tuning" IRA contributions. Look for greater IRA deductibility as well as increased contributions in the next few years.

MISCELLANEOUS

There are several miscellaneous deductible items. The cost of professional fees that are incurred in connection with your tax return preparation or tax consulting is deductible. Costs of *carrying investments* may be deductible including subscriptions to various publications. Your safe deposit box annual fee is deductible if it's used to hold income-producing investments documents, i.e., stocks that pay dividends or interest. Portions of your home may be deductible, but they must be used exclusively for the purpose of the business or a place of business that is used by patients, clients or customers in meeting or dealing with you. If you use a home office and are employed by someone else, the related cost is not deductible unless the home office is required by your employer and he or she puts it in writing.

If the above items exceed 2 percent of your AGI, then they can be included as itemized deductions.

CHILD CARE

If you pay for child care, a portion of the cost can be treated as a credit. Most people are not aware there is a difference between a tax deduction and a tax credit. A deduction reduces your taxable income before the actual tax is determined. A tax credit is subtracted from the actual amount of taxes you owe. The maximum child care credit for one child is $720, for two or more, $1,440.

If you earn $10,000 a year or less, you will be allowed to take up to 30 percent of your child care cost up to $2,400. If you have one child, a maximum of $720 ($2,400 × 30 percent = $720); for two children, $1,440 ($4,800 × 30 percent = $1,440).

The amount you will be able to claim as a credit will be calculated on a sliding scale. For families who earn in excess of $28,000 a year, the percentage drops to 20 percent. This means that if you have one child, your credit will be $480 ($2,400 × 20 percent = $480) and if you have two or more children, $960 ($4,800 × 20 percent = $960). Any amount you spend in excess of $2,400 for a single child or $4,800 for two or more, is not included in the calculation and is merely an expensed item.

The W-4 and you. Legitimate deductions offer one area for tax savings; efficient manipulation of the W-4 withholding form is another. The problem is few people bother to read it. In fact, most merely count themselves and dependents, if they have any, as the only withholding allowance for payroll purposes.

If you get a refund at the end of each year, you are losing a lot of money. You are providing a 12-month plus interest-free loan to the government with monies you could be using. It is simply not necessary to have huge amounts withheld from your paycheck, if you have the proper deductions to back up a lesser withholding figure.

Now, the instructions on the W-4 form are fairly explicit. They do tell you not to overwithhold or underwithhold. The odds are that if you receive a check in excess of $200, the withholding sum is too great. In the old days, pre-1982, the IRS would send out a notice suggesting you change your withholding declarations so a refund wouldn't be sent in the future. It no longer does.

Today's W-4 consists of two pages. Neither are complicated and can be completed within 30 minutes *if* you know what your deductions will be—home mortgage interest, the allowable percentage of personal interest, charitable contributions, state and local taxes (no sales tax), medical expenses in excess of 7.5 percent of your income, and miscellaneous deductions (most miscellaneous deductions are now deductible only in excess of 2 percent of your income). If you don't know the exact numbers (nobody will until after the year has ended) keep in mind that this is an estimate—when in doubt use last year's tax return as a guide.

Do yourself a favor and calculate twice a year what your overall tax liability will be. If you withhold at least 90 percent of what your obligation is, you will incur no penalties. People the IRS identify as "tax protestors," or others who deliberately understate their withholdings will be hit with a $500 penalty.

Let's do a sample W-4. Both sides of the form have been duplicated. Assume you are a two-income couple with two children and a total income of $55,000 plus $1,000 in interest earned. Your spouse earns $30,000 a year and you earn $25,000. Your itemized deductions total $14,400 and alimony paid to a former spouse is $4,800 a year. Contributions of $4,000 are made to IRAs for both husband and wife. You also pay $2,400 a year in child care expenses. Since your adjusted gross income is over $50,000, the IRAs will not be included as an adjustment to income. If you had no itemized deductions, nor received income from other sources, you would merely complete the first page relating to the *Personal Allowances Worksheet.*

With the above "couple" as an example, both sides of the worksheet would be completed. Here's how:

Personal Allowances Worksheet, page 1
A. for your personal dependent exemption, enter "1";

B. if you are single or married, but only one of you works outside the home or if married, your spouse's wages (or the total of both) are less than $2,500, enter "1";

C. if you are married, enter "1" if spouse does not declare self on his or her W-4;

D. enter number of dependents other than self and spouse—you have "2";

E. enter "0", you are not head of household;

F. if you have child care or dependent expenses in excess of $1,500, this line is completed—you do, claim "1";

G. add lines A through F—your total is "5".

The remainder of the *Employee's Withholding Allowance Certificate* will be completed after the *Deductions and Adjustments Worksheet* on page 2 is completed.

1. enter your estimated itemized deductions amount of $14,400;

2. enter $5,450 for married filing jointly;

3. subtract line 2 from line 1 (14,400-5,450=8,950) and enter 8,950;

4. enter adjustments to income of 4,800—alimony and IRAs (since adjusted gross income is over $50,000, IRAs can't be deducted);

5. add lines 3 and 4 (8,950+4,800=13,750), enter 13,750;

6. enter estimate of earned income (interest, dividends), 1,000;

7. subtract line 6 from line 5, enter 12,750 (13,750-1,000=12,750);

8. divide line 7 by 2,000—eliminate fractions, enter 6 (12,750÷2,000=6.375);

9. enter 5, the number from side one, *Personal Allowances Worksheet,* line G;

10. add lines 8 and 9, enter 11 (6 + 5 = 11); if you use the next worksheet on page 2 (the *Two-Earner/Two-Job Worksheet*), also enter the total on its line 1.

Two-Earner/Two-Job Worksheet
1. enter the number from line G on page 1 or from line 10 from the *Deductions and Adjustments Worksheet* above—5;

2. from Table 1 on the worksheet, find the number that applies to the LOWEST paying job ($25,000), which is 4;

3. subtract line 2 from line 1 (5-4 = 1) and enter 1.
   Now, go back to the first page and enter your totals on the *Employee's Withholding Allowance Certificate* (section 4) for a total of 16 allowances along with your name and address (section 1), Social Security number (section 2) marital status (section 3). Complete section 5 if you want any additional funds withheld, section 6 if you qualify to have NO additional withholding and section 7 if you are a full-time student. Sign and date the certificate, your employer will complete the remainder relating to his or her identification for IRS purposes.

Sound easy and nonconfusing? Of course not. No one said taxes were simple or easy. They are, though, guaranteed to be with us for our lifetimes in some form or another. Your job is to make sure you pay your share—but your fair share only!

1990 Form W-4

 Department of the Treasury
Internal Revenue Service

Purpose. Complete Form W-4 so that your employer can withhold the correct amount of Federal income tax from your pay.

Exemption From Withholding. Read line 6 of the certificate below to see if you can claim exempt status. *If exempt, complete line 6; but do not complete lines 4 and 5.* No Federal income tax will be withheld from your pay. This exemption expires February 15, 1991.

Basic Instructions. Employees who are not exempt should complete the Personal Allowances Worksheet. Additional worksheets are provided on page 2 for employees to adjust their withholding allowances based on itemized deductions, adjustments to income, or two-earner/two-job situations. Complete all worksheets that apply to your situation. The worksheets will help you figure the number of withholding allowances you are

entitled to claim. However, you may claim fewer allowances than this.

Head of Household. Generally, you may claim head of household filing status on your tax return only if you are unmarried and pay more than 50% of the costs of keeping up a home for yourself and your dependent(s) or other qualifying individuals.

Nonwage Income. If you have a large amount of nonwage income, such as interest or dividends, you should consider making estimated tax payments using Form 1040-ES. Otherwise, you may find that you owe additional tax at the end of the year.

Two-Earner/Two-Jobs. If you have a working spouse or more than one job, figure the total number of allowances you are entitled to claim on all jobs using worksheets from only one Form

W-4. This total should be divided among all jobs. Your withholding will usually be most accurate when all allowances are claimed on the W-4 filed for the highest paying job and zero allowances are claimed for the others.

Advance Earned Income Credit. If you are eligible for this credit, you can receive it added to your paycheck throughout the year. For details, obtain Form W-5 from your employer.

Check Your Withholding. After your W-4 takes effect, you can use Publication 919, Is My Withholding Correct for 1990?, to see how the dollar amount you are having withheld compares to your estimated total annual tax. Call 1-800-424-3676 (in Hawaii and Alaska, check your local telephone directory) to order this publication. Check your local telephone directory for the IRS assistance number if you need further help.

Personal Allowances Worksheet

A Enter "1" for **yourself** if no one else can claim you as a dependent . . . . **A** _1_

B Enter "1" if:
1. You are single and have only one job; or
2. You are married, have only one job, and your spouse does not work; or
3. Your wages from a second job or your spouse's wages (or the total of both) are $2,500 or less. . . . . **B** ____

C Enter "1" for your **spouse.** But, you may choose to enter "0" if you are married and have either a working spouse or more than one job (this may help you avoid having too little tax withheld) . . . . **C** _1_

D Enter number of **dependents** (other than your spouse or yourself) whom you will claim on your tax return . . . . **D** _2_

E Enter "1" if you will file as a **head of household** on your tax return (see conditions under "Head of Household," above) . **E** ____

F Enter "1" if you have at least $1,500 of **child or dependent care expenses** for which you plan to claim a credit . . . **F** _1_

G Add lines A through F and enter total here . . . . ▶ **G** _5_

For accuracy, do all worksheets that apply.
- If you plan to **itemize or claim adjustments to income** and want to reduce your withholding, turn to the Deductions and Adjustments Worksheet on page 2.
- If you are **single** and have **more than one job** and your combined earnings from all jobs exceed $25,000 OR if you are **married** and have a **working spouse or more than one job,** and the combined earnings from all jobs exceed $44,000, then turn to the Two-Earner/Two-Job Worksheet on page 2 if you want to avoid having too little tax withheld.

● If neither of the above situations applies to you, **stop here** and enter the number from line G on line 4 of Form W-4 below.

-------- Cut here and give the certificate to your employer. Keep the top portion for your records. --------

| **Form W-4** Department of the Treasury Internal Revenue Service | **Employee's Withholding Allowance Certificate** ▶ For Privacy Act and Paperwork Reduction Act Notice, see reverse. | OMB No. 1545-0010 19**90** |

1 Type or print your first name and middle initial *Johnson*   Last name *Roberta*

2 Your social security number *555-55-5555*

Home address (number and street or rural route) *123 Main St.*

City or town, state, and ZIP code *Anywhere*

3 Marital status

☐ Single ☒ Married

☐ Married, but withhold at higher Single rate.

Note: *If married, but legally separated, or spouse is a nonresident alien, check the Single box.*

4 Total number of allowances you are claiming (from line G above or from the Worksheets on back if they apply) . . . . | **4** | *16* |

5 Additional amount, if any, you want deducted from each pay . . . . | **5** $ | |

6 I claim exemption from withholding and I certify that I meet **ALL** of the following conditions for exemption:
- Last year I had a right to a refund of **ALL** Federal income tax withheld because I had **NO** tax liability; **AND**
- This year I expect a refund of **ALL** Federal income tax withheld because I expect to have **NO** tax liability; **AND**
- This year if my income exceeds $500 and includes nonwage income, another person cannot claim me as a dependent.

If you meet all of the above conditions, enter the year effective and "EXEMPT" here ▶ **6** | 19 |

7 Are you a full-time student? (**Note:** *Full-time students are not automatically exempt.*) . . . . . **7** ☐ Yes ☒ No

Under penalties of perjury, I certify that I am entitled to the number of withholding allowances claimed on this certificate or entitled to claim exempt status.

Employee's signature ▶ *Roberta Johnson*   Date ▶ *1-12* , 19 *90*

8 Employer's name and address (Employer: Complete 8 and 10 only if sending to IRS) | **9** Office code (optional) | **10** Employer identification number |

Cowdery's Form No. 1505 (1/90)

Deductions and Adjustments Worksheet

Note: *Use this worksheet only if you plan to itemize deductions or claim adjustments to income on your 1990 tax return.*

1 Enter an estimate of your 1990 itemized deductions. These include: qualifying home mortgage interest, 10% of personal interest, charitable contributions, state and local taxes (but not sales taxes), medical expenses in excess of 7.5% of your income, and miscellaneous deductions (most miscellaneous deductions are now deductible only in excess of 2% of your income) . . . . **1** $ *14,400*

2 Enter: $5,450 if married filing jointly or qualifying widow(er)
         $4,750 if head of household
         $3,250 if single
         $2,725 if married filing separately . . . . **2** $ *5,450*

3 **Subtract** line 2 from line 1. If line 2 is greater than line 1, enter zero . . . . **3** $ *8,950*

4 Enter an estimate of your 1990 adjustments to income. These include alimony paid and deductible IRA contributions . . **4** $ *4,800*

5 **Add** lines 3 and 4 and enter the total . . . . **5** $ *13,750*

6 Enter an estimate of your 1990 nonwage income (such as dividends or interest income) . . . **6** $ *1,000*

7 **Subtract** line 6 from line 5. Enter the result, but not less than zero . . . . **7** $ *12,750*

8 **Divide** the amount on line 7 by $2,000 and enter the result here. Drop any fraction **8** *6*

9 Enter the number from Personal Allowances Worksheet, line G, on page 1 . . . . **9** *5*

10 **Add** lines 8 and 9 and enter the total here. If you plan to use the Two-Earner/Two-Job Worksheet, also enter the total on line 1, below. Otherwise, **stop here** and enter this total on Form W-4, line 4 on page 1 . . . **10** *11*

Two-Earner/Two-Job Worksheet

Note: *Use this worksheet only if the instructions at line G on page 1 direct you here.*

1 Enter the number from line G on page 1 (or from line 10 above if you used the Deductions and Adjustments Worksheet) . **1** *5*

2 Find the number in **Table 1** below that applies to the **LOWEST** paying job and enter it here **2** *4*

3 If line 1 is **GREATER THAN OR EQUAL TO** line 2, subtract line 2 from line 1. Enter the result here (if zero, enter "0") and on Form W-4, line 4, on page 1. **DO NOT** use the rest of this worksheet **3** *1*

Note: *If line 1 is LESS THAN line 2, enter "0" on Form W-4, line 4, on page 1. Complete lines 4–9 to calculate the additional dollar withholding necessary to avoid a year-end tax bill.*

4 Enter the number from line 2 of this worksheet **4**

5 Enter the number from line 1 of this worksheet **5**

6 Subtract line 5 from line 4 . . . . **6**

7 Find the amount in **Table 2** below that applies to the **HIGHEST** paying job and enter it here . . . . **7** $

8 **Multiply** line 7 by line 6 and enter the result here. This is the additional annual withholding amount needed **8** $

9 Divide line 8 by the number of pay periods each year. (For example, divide by 26 if you are paid every other week.) Enter the result here and on Form W-4, line 5, page 1. This is the additional amount to be withheld from each paycheck . . **9** $

Table 1: Two-Earner/Two-Job Worksheet

Married Filing Jointly		All Others	
If wages from LOWEST paying job are—	Enter on line 2 above	If wages from LOWEST paying job are—	Enter on line 2 above
0 - $4,000	0	0 - $4,000	0
4,001 - 8,000	1	4,001 - 8,000	1
8,001 - 19,000	2	8,001 - 14,000	2
19,001 - 23,000	3	14,001 - 16,000	3
23,001 - 25,000	4	16,001 - 21,000	4
25,001 - 27,000	5	21,001 and over	5
27,001 - 29,000	6		
29,001 - 35,000	7		
35,001 - 41,000	8		
41,001 - 46,000	9		
46,001 and over	10		

Table 2: Two-Earner/Two-Job Worksheet

Married Filing Jointly		All Others	
If wages from HIGHEST paying job are—	Enter on line 7 above	If wages from HIGHEST paying job are—	Enter on line 7 above
0 - $44,000	$310	0 - $25,000	$310
44,001 - 90,000	570	25,001 - 52,000	570
90,001 and over	680	52,001 and over	680

Privacy Act and Paperwork Reduction Act Notice.—We ask for this information to carry out the Internal Revenue laws of the United States. We may give the information to the Department of Justice for civil or criminal litigation and to cities, states, and the District of Columbia for use in administering their tax laws. You are required to give this information to your employer.

The time needed to complete this form will vary depending on individual circumstances. The estimated average time is: **Recordkeeping** 46 min., **Learning about the law or the form** 10 min., **Preparing the form** 70 min. If you have comments concerning the accuracy of these time estimates or suggestions for making this form more simple, we would be happy to hear from you. You can write to the **Internal Revenue Service**, Washington, DC 20224, Attn: IRS Reports Clearance Officer, T:FP; or the **Office of Management and Budget**, Paperwork Reduction Project (1545-0010), Washington, DC 20503.

*U.S. Government Printing Office 1989-245-083

A SHELTER IS A SHELTER

Although it has a slightly disreputable ring, a tax shelter is simply by definition any enterprise into which you invest money expecting to realize a profit and receive some form of tax benefit at the same time. Unless you go through life paying minimal taxes, you will probably at some time or another participate in some form of tax shelter. Your home is the most common one. One reason owning may be cheaper than renting is that you can deduct the interest on a mortgage, as well as any related property taxes.

Other shelters could include investment real estate, as well as various business ventures. They can have many functions. One is deferral of income. Another is substantial write-off. A third is income sheltered through depreciation. A fourth is equity building.

In the best of circumstances, tax shelters can supply tax breaks substantial enough so that tax pressured individuals will focus only on the pluses and ignore the drawbacks. It is important to remember the object here is to make money. Tax shelters are not *low risk* and there is no sense in avoiding taxes at the expense of your capital. Otherwise, you would be far better off to make a sizable contribution to your favorite charity, receive a 100 percent deduction and sleep well at night. A shelter must still be a quality investment first and always. Study your particular situation and get good professional advice before investing in any.

Although the tax laws are ever changing, supposedly toward simplification, the opportunities discussed for tax savings will always be appropriate. Sound financial planning and stewardship will require tax consideration.

CHAPTER SIX

Selective Indebtedness—Or Giving Credit That's Due

Within the Christian tradition, debt is considered a negative condition, an *economic bondage* that saps energy, undermines optimism and precludes faith. After all, Proverbs 22:7 cautions, "Just as the rich rule the poor, so the borrower is servant to the lender." But credit is not necessarily the same as debt, and life is no longer as physically simplistic as it was when Proverbs was written.

Certainly, creating unmanageable debt is foolish, even destructive. But using debt or credit as a tool in a long-term cogent financial plan is smart. It is wise and sound financial management.

Using your assets to your best advantage includes learning to take full advantage of the credit your net worth and earning power entitle you to. The rich may still rule the poor, but the borrower no longer need be slave to anyone, much less the lender.

Credit takes on many different forms. It has applications and implications on both short- and long-term bases.

The key is to understand and use credit wisely; to heed the words of Luke when he wrote, "But don't begin until you count the cost. For who would begin construction of a building without first getting estimates and then checking to see if he has enough money to pay the bills?" (Luke 14:28).

CREDIT IS A FACT OF LIFE

Credit is an inescapable part of modern life. All of us at one time or another will have to acquire money from an outside

---

If credit is used properly, it can be your friend, not your foe.

---

source. You can use credit to improve your situation, provided you act wisely and make good use of another economic phenomenon—borrowing. If you ask most people what they use banks for, they would probably tell you for a checking or savings account. Both are items in which money is deposited with the bank. Have you ever thought what would happen if the bank were merely a depository. It would go out of business. In order for a bank to succeed, it must also lend money.

The days of the 1970s and early '80s were crazy with high inflation. A dramatic increase in consumer credit abounded. Everyone had credit cards, some too many. Bankers were openly soliciting loans to customers and potential new customers that were unsecured. This means they would loan money without having anything as collateral, such as a car, home, business or savings account.

Most Christians have been taught that borrowing is bad. Many believe the use of credit cards and even buying on any form of credit is sinful. Now, coveting material items not needed or affordable is a sin. Too much credit is easily misused and can have devastating results. And many may find they have trouble controlling their spending when it's so easy to present that all-too-familiar card. But if credit is used properly, it can be your friend, not your foe.

A Proper Introduction

The proper use of credit is a step toward proper stewardship. It can work to accelerate your net worth, balancing the effects of inflation. At the same time, it can also make your life easier and more comfortable, freeing and giving you more energy and more assets to devote to Christian priorities.

No Christian would deny the value of saving money. But how many of you have considered that credit is like savings? Having credit available is similar to having savings in a bank. If you had taken the trouble to establish some credit rating by buying on time and paying off on time; if you had focused on building a proper relationship with the bank manager over the years and demonstrated you are a good, responsible citizen with stable employment or ability to repay, the bank would be delighted to lend $5,000 on an unsecured basis. Having that *ability* to borrow $5,000 has the same effect as having $5,000 in the bank. It's there in case you need it. It's there for the rainy day, and you retain use of the cash itself.

That same reasoning applies to credit cards. What credit cards represent is the ability to obtain cash, goods or services. They sometimes take the place of savings, if needed. I am sure you know someone who has lost their job or had a sudden financial burden hit them. They had no cash to pay for ongoing living expenses until they turned themselves around. Many never know how bad off they are financially until it's nearly too late. Having credit cards that have been paid regularly and on time can act as that *savings* if such a disaster hits. It doesn't mean you rush out and run them up, buying extravagant presents or borrowing the cash advances that carries an expensive interest cost. All it means is that it's there for that rainy day, if your savings are exhausted—if all else fails.

Let the Talents Be Your Guide

Savings sometimes become the least best alternative. The best alternative, in my opinion, is having your money out there working and multiplying as the Parable of the Talents tells us.

Credit cards can actually help build a strong arsenal and personal financial plan. Some cards can be obtained for free, others have annual charges. Five years ago it was common for people to have many credit cards in their wallets and purses. Today that's changed. With technology and the dual acceptance of many stores and vendors for credit cards other than their own, the Christian woman doesn't need to carry or possess lots of cards. A Visa and MasterCard make sense, as well as one of the business cards such as American Express, Diners Club, Carte Blanche or the Discover Card. Visa and MasterCard have limitations on how much can be charged, American Express does not have limitations, as long as your bill is paid off in full at the time of its receipt.

If you travel, a business card is vital, especially for your airline tickets. Major stores such as Macys and J.C. Penney take the American Express card. Sears, the nation's largest retailer, introduced its Discover Card in 1986. It's like a super-duper MasterCard, acceptable at retailers other than Sears; it gives its holder the ability to withdraw cash at any Sears store, as well as specific Automatic Teller Machines located throughout the United States.

Credit cards can also be used to keep track of different types of payments. You may have some expenses that are tax deductible or business related. Put those on your Visa card. Your personal expenses can be placed on your MasterCard or vice versa. The credit card companies send a detailed statement at the end of the billing period stating where you spent the money, as well as the establishment, such as a restaurant. It's a useful and detailed list of transactions completed in any given month.

Warning Ahead!

A word of caution here: Beware of the danger of running too many charges that cannot be paid off when your bill comes. In order to avoid any finance charges, your credit card statements must be paid in full before the due date. What you have done is used the issuing card company's money for a short period of time to purchase the goods or services you needed. This is called "float."

Be sure you know what the billing cycle of your card is. It is usually noted on your statement as the billing period. Charges and payments received after that date will be noted on the next month's statement. If you have to buy any major item, purchase it right after that date; it will give you a longer period before you have to pay the funds back. Your statement, which reflects the purchase, will not come until the following month. Normally you have several days after receiving the statement before payment is due. When bills state a specific date due, it is common to have a grace period, 7-10 days after the due date, to actually pay your bill before your payment is considered late.

With this strategy of buying right after the billing period, not paying until after you receive the next statement and taking advantage of the grace period, you have benefited from six to seven weeks of float time. Over a period of time, this can add up to a significant amount of money. It is far smarter than paying 18 to 21 percent on outstanding credit card balances. You stretch your budget further and justify the annual credit card cost.

Not a New Idea

The concept of using another's money to make a profit is not new. In fact, the banks have made an art of it. They have routinely floated on your checking account, your savings account, even at the time they release funds that have been tied up in one of their certificate of deposit accounts.

Under current banking policy, funds deposited into a checking account can be withdrawn immediately. Rarely is that done. Normally the funds are deposited into the checking account, and as checks are written against the balance, they are disbursed. Sometimes it takes a few days, sometimes many weeks.

Most banks have thousands of accounts. Imagine how much money is accumulated in this process. The bank knows that all of the funds are not going to be withdrawn at once. After all, they have a history to go by. They now have at their disposal hundreds of thousands of dollars on a very short-term basis.

Funds are pooled or combined and loaned to others. Loans can range from a few days to many months. Since

---

A good credit rating will give you leverage, or the ability for the calculated use of credit so that you may use other people's money to make money for yourself, just like the banks do.

---

funds are continuously coming in as new deposits in both checking and savings, it appears the bank never runs out of money. They make it a practice that no funds sit around doing nothing, not even overnight. Every day counts to a bank's earning capabilities. It should to yours too.

Hold Up

Have you ever deposited a check into your account that was received from a friend as a gift? Unfortunately, your friend lives in another state. The bank puts a hold on your check. The teller explains your funds are not available to use for anywhere from 3 to 10 days until the check clears.

With modern banking and the technology available, most checks clear within a 48-hour period. Even though the check that was written to you and deposited was paid by the issuing bank from the other state, you still haven't use of your funds until that hold period is up. If you are a regular customer of the bank, any hold greater than 3 days is too much in my opinion. Talk to the manager—there are other banks that would welcome your business.

DO YOU HAVE LEVERAGE?

This leads us to another aspect of credit: establishing a solid credit rating for you and the members of your family. A good credit rating will give you leverage, or the ability for the calculated use of credit so that you may use other people's money to make money for yourself, just like the banks do.

Leverage is, in fact, a very apt word if you remember anything from your high school science classes. A lever allows you to exert a far greater effort than the actual force used. It can be used to lift an object you couldn't ordinarily budge. In the financial sense, it means you are able to purchase items you might not be able to afford if you used assets such as cash currently on hand. If used wisely, leverage can work to increase the overall growth of your net worth. The flip side, of course, is you can overdo it. You do not want to find yourself in the position that at the end of the month the payments required to meet your obligations exceed the actual income you have available to make them.

If you find your money runs out before the end of the month, even after adjusting withholding taxes that could increase your monthly cash flow and identifying all possible sources of income, you have a problem. If you are unable to meet your monthly cash flow obligations, you are clearly overleveraged.

CREDIT TALKS, WHO LISTENS?

If you haven't received a copy of your credit report, get one at once. Make it an annual ritual—just to see what is being said and shared about you to merchants and financial institutions who query the reporting agencies. Have you ever received a credit card in the mail, out of the blue, without applying for it? Or, have you ever been turned down when you've applied?

One of my daughters was rejected for a car loan; the creditor's reason was that she couldn't possibly make payments based on her earnings and existing amounts owed on other obligations *and* that she hadn't reported all her outstanding debts. Sheryl was puzzled and angry. She had reported everything.

Finally, the mystery was solved. Sheryl requested a copy of her report and guess what?! She found her older sister's accounts reported as hers, as well as one of mine. Of course she couldn't handle three people's obligations! It took a month to unravel the mess. The end result—she got her loan.

Don't go through what Sheryl did. Preventive action is called for. By obtaining a copy of your report prior to applying for credit, you have the opportunity to correct errors. And they do happen, often.

When you have been rejected on a credit application, you have from 30 days to 6 months to get a copy of your report, free of charge. Length of time will vary, depending on the reporting agencies policies in your area.

Action Plan

If you've been rejected, return a copy of your denial letter to the reporting agency with a request for a copy of your report. The address of the reporting agency will be on the denial letter. If it's within the "free period," a full credit report will be sent to you. You now have the opportunity to make corrections *or* to make a statement as to what caused you to be late on a payment, for example. It will be entered on your report. You can even direct the agency to send corrected reports to merchants who have made inquiries. Their names will appear on your report as an "inquiry."

If you haven't been rejected, but want to find out what your report says, contact the reporting agency in your area. Look in the Yellow Pages under Credit Reporting Agencies. The largest is TRW, Inc. Others include CBI or Credit Bureau Inc. and TransUnion. The cost to you will be approximately $15.

The agency will tell you to send in specific information with your identification (Social Security number, address, former address, full name, employer, and so on) and a check for the service charge. Within a few weeks, you will have a copy of your report, usually in duplicate. If you find any errors (which is not unusual), correct one of the copies and/or include a letter of explanation and return the altered copy to the agency who sent it. By law, they must check out all disputes.

Another way to probe deeper, and quicker, is to work with a service that can supply additional information—such as the phone numbers and your specific account number with the creditor. This gives you a "one-up" and allows you to go straight to the reporting source with a phone call. Many people find that accounts have been opened they knew nothing about—remember, there are plenty of John and Jane Smiths out there! Credit-VU in San Jose, California charges $25 for a detailed report with phone numbers and account numbers within 24-hours of your written request. You can contact them at 1-800-594-5969. It is definitely worth the extra $10 for greater detail and speed.

Even if you don't "charge" items, some form of credit reporting still occurs if you have a home mortgage, car payment or gas card. Many landlords do a credit check on prospective renters. If you need to rent a car, reserve a hotel room, order airline tickets—you will need a credit card to back you up until you arrive with the cash.

If you think your credit is outstanding, it is still wise to check out what is in the "system" about you and/or your spouse. Names are similar. Social Security numbers a digit apart. Mistakes are made daily. Call and request a copy of what is being reported about you. Today.

USING CREDIT TO EARN MONEY

How do you use credit to earn money? Simply stated, you purchase something with someone else's money, let it appreciate, then sell it at a profit.

Let's take a mythical $100,000 house and assume you have the $20,000 necessary for the down payment. Your credit report, net worth statement and earnings capabilities satisfies the lender, who then advances you the additional $80,000 needed to buy the house. In turn, you agree to pay interest on the money you are using, eventually paying off the principal amount if you own the house the entire period of the loan. Most home loans are for 30 years, although 15 years has become common. That in itself is simple leverage. But let's take it a step further.

Assume that not only are you able to convince the bank to lend you the $80,000, but also that you have a second source willing to put up an additional $10,000. You can use that $10,000 for part of the down payment on the home, or you can put it in a savings account for a rainy day fund.

Over a three-year period, the house has appreciated to

$150,000; you decide to sell it. The closing costs and commissions will reduce the proceeds to $138,000. From that amount, subtract $80,000 (very little will be paid down over the three years toward the principal amount), subtract an additional $10,000 to repay the $10,000 you borrowed for a portion of the down payment, or for your rainy day funds, and subtract the other $10,000 you put up for the original purchase. Your profit is $38,000 from the initial outlay of just $10,000 from your own resources—a net return of 380 percent over three years.

$150,000	sales price
-12,000	closing costs and commissions
$138,000	gross proceeds
-80,000	bank loan
-10,000	second trust deed
-10,000	down payment (personal)
$ 38,000	profit

$38,000 ÷ $10,000 = 380% return

If you had not borrowed the additional $10,000, your personal outlay would have been $20,000. The overall return on your $20,000 would still be $38,000, or a 190 percent return.

$150,000	sales price
-12,000	closing costs and commissions
$138,000	gross proceeds
-80,000	bank loan
-20,000	down payment (personal)
$ 38,000	profit

$38,000 ÷ $20,000 = 190% return

These two illustrations juggle figures since the eventual cash out is the same in either case. But let's take it a step further. Suppose after borrowing from the second lender to make half your down payment, you took the additional $10,000 that was left over in your personal account and put it to work in another profitable investment. Let's say you found another, smaller home costing $50,000 that you could rent out. With the 20 percent down payment, or $10,000, the rental income you would receive from the property would more than likely cover the mortgage payments. If it, like the first home, appreciates 50 percent in three years, it will be worth $75,000 when you sell it. Even with the closing costs and commissions on the second house (assume 8 percent of sales price), you will show a handsome profit of approximately $19,000 on your initial $10,000 investment.

$75,000	sales price
- 6,000	closing costs and commissions
$69,000	gross proceeds
-40,000	bank loan
-10,000	down payment (personal)
$ 19,000	profit

$19,000 ÷ $10,000 = 190% return

Now, leverage has really begun to work for you. In each illustration, you began with the same $20,000 cash in an account. In the first example, you used the full amount as a down payment. Your profit from the single home over the three years was $38,000. In the second example, you used only part of the credit available to you. In the final example, leverage had been used to the maximum. Not only did you leverage yourself with the original $80,000 loan from the bank, but also in the $10,000 that was borrowed from the second lender and the $40,000 mortgage that was taken out to pay for the second home.

Your gross profit before any tax consideration is $57,000 ($38,000 + $19,000) versus $38,000. But in each case, the sum of initial capital was the same.

A Roof Over Someone Else's Head

Now let's take it a step further. The advantage of leverage is even more dramatically illustrated in another example. I have often said that the art of leverage is in using credit to the maximum without exceeding your overall ability to make the payments. In this case, the income from the purchase of rental properties will provide most of that means. The tax advantages from the payment of interest will be presumed to cover the rest. These projections, plus the fact the investment will be protected by the 20 percent down payment on the property, will convince the bank to lend a substantial amount of money.

Let's say your Great-aunt Martha has left you $100,000. With that money, you purchase a single family home and pay all cash. There is no mortgage; you therefore have no leverage. It's safe to project the property can appreciate 10 percent per year and that you follow the progress of the home's value in the chart that follows. After a year, the property is worth $110,000 ($100,000 + 10 percent of $100,000). After the second year, the value has increased to $121,000 ($110,000 + 10 percent of $110,000). After five years, the value of the property has climbed to $161,051. If you decide to sell at this period, your gross profit would be $61,051. Adjusting by approximately 8 percent for selling costs and commissions of $12,884, your net profit will be approximately $48,167, or a 48 percent return.

Suppose, though, that instead of buying the house for $100,000 cash, you use the money for four down payments of $20,000 each on homes costing $100,000. Instead of one house increasing 10 percent per year, you have four houses each originally valued at $100,000 and each increasing at 10 percent per year. The fifth $20,000 will be used as a cash reserve to help supplement rents that are received, which, in turn, will allow you to make your mortgage payments.

By the end of the first year alone, the equity in the four homes will total $120,000—nearly two-thirds the increased value of the single home after a five-year period! Equity is the value of the home in excess of any indebtedness against it. At the end of the second year, equity in the four homes totals $164,000, and by the end of the fifth year, when the four homes are sold for $161,051 each, your equity has increased to $324,204.

From that amount, subtract the original $100,000 that you started with and $51,536 that represents 8 percent of the combined sales prices of $644,204. Your profit is $172,668 or approximately 173 percent.

Now let's consider the inflation factor that seems to be with the real estate market in perpetuity. Over the five years, the $48,167 profit from the single house barely offsets the effects of a 9 percent inflation factor on the original $100,000. With the purchase of four homes, there is a much greater cushion against the ravages of inflation.

In these illustrations, I have not allowed for a small

reduction in the mortgage principal due to the greater proportion of monthly payments allocated to interest in the first few years.

In addition, I have not taken into consideration the tax advantages received by the owner from interest payments, real estate taxes, various expenses and depreciation. In real estate investments, one of the greatest areas of tax advantages comes from depreciation. To the investor, this could mean a greater reduction in tax obligations, further enhancing the rate of return.

With our ever-changing tax laws and tax reform, it is critical for any investor, especially in the real estate area, to keep current with tax laws. What's good today may not necessarily be good tomorrow. The motto "Be prepared" is certainly appropriate here.

A FINAL WORD

As you can see, credit is not necessarily a *bad guy*. Credit can be part of the "good soil" that Mark writes about that enables seeds to bear fruit 30-fold and 60-fold and 100-fold (see Mark 4:20). Borrowed money can be used to purchase anything from new clothes to a long-awaited home. But it also can be used to make more money—to purchase something with somebody else's money, let it appreciate, then sell it for a profit.

When you begin to use credit, have your facts available. Make sure your credit rating is in order, that you have the ability to repay and that you are realistic about your needs and roles. Proverbs gives ample warning about

Investment 1:

All cash—increasing in value by 10% per year

Investment 2:

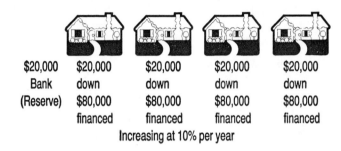

| $20,000 Bank (Reserve) | $20,000 down $80,000 financed | $20,000 down $80,000 financed | $20,000 down $80,000 financed | $20,000 down $80,000 financed |

Increasing at 10% per year

		Market Value	Mortgage	Equity
Year 1:	4 houses @ $110,000 = $440,000		$320,000	$120,000
2:	4 houses @ $121,000 = $484,000		$320,000	$164,000
3:	4 houses @ $133,100 = $532,400		$320,000	$212,400
4:	4 houses @ $146,410 = $585,640		$320,000	$265,640
5:	4 houses @ $161,051 = $644,204		$320,000	$324,204

	Investment 1	Investment 2
Current market value:	$161,051	$644,204
Profit (Increased dollar value over original $100,000, after 8% deduction for closing costs and commissions:$48,167	$172,668	
Percentage Return:	48%	173%

being prepared, "The wise man looks ahead. The fool attempts to fool himself and won't face facts" (Prov. 14:8) and "It is dangerous and sinful to rush into the unknown" (19:2).

Throughout the New Testament is the additional message that God does not want us to rest on our laurels. "Don't be misled; remember that you can't ignore God and get away with it: a man will always reap just the kind of crop he sows!" (Gal. 6:7).

So will a woman!

CHAPTER SEVEN
Kids and Money

Having children adds a new dimension to your financial picture, as well as your personal life. Their impact on your financial game plan cannot be ignored. Children are a responsibility, and providing for your family is both a joy and an obligation. "Anyone who won't care for his own relatives when they need help, especially those living in his own family, has no right to say he is a Christian. Such a person is worse than the heathen" (1 Tim. 5:8).

Providing for your family basically means planning ahead. "A sensible man watches for problems ahead and prepares to meet them. The simpleton never looks, and suffers the consequences" (Prov. 27:12).

PLAN AHEAD!

A prudent plan for managing your income must now include monies for unforeseen emergencies, savings for education (particularly college) and ways of seeding dreams for your children. If children are new in your life, it's a good idea to examine a cash flow analysis of your income and anticipated expenses to see if you need to change your spending habits.

Though your greatest expenses are still in the future (underwriting the teenage and college years), the routine costs of infancy are a surprise for most new parents. Even normal hospital delivery and initial pediatrician costs can bankrupt you if you don't plan ahead. My first grandchild arrived in the spring of 1987. The hospital bill alone was just shy of $4,000—for a normal delivery! Most of the bill was covered by insurance, but what if it hadn't been?

Child Care

Child care is another big expense. Under current law, two-income couples and single working parents can claim a tax credit for a portion of these child care costs, which is subtracted from any federal income taxes owed. You should also check employee benefit plans because some have provisions that augment child care costs.

Emergency Funds

With kids, it's especially important to keep an emergency reserve fund of from three to six months of ongoing living expenses in safe, liquid vehicles, such as money market funds or short-term insured certificates of deposit. And finally, those college expenses I spoke of will come due all too soon. To help prepare you, some financial institutions can provide a personalized analysis of what your child's education might cost and what you can do now to meet those future bills.

Education Note

A side note may be in order here. As I write, various concepts are being bantered about for guaranteed tuition programs. In Michigan, the Michigan Education Trust is truly innovative. The first of its kind, it will permit parents of kids any age, even newborns, to pay now as little as $3,000 for four years of tuition later at any of the state's 15 public colleges or 29 community colleges. The amount paid will be dependent on how close enrollment is. Other states are eyeing the concept with over half of state legislatures considering comparable programs. Formal implementation of Michigan's program is expected when a tax exempt status is issued by the IRS.

If your objective is to provide a college education for your children, I encourage you to write your state representative and support Michigan's concept. Why not have it where you live too? Today's cost for one year of tuition, books, room and board, is equivalent to what a small house cost 30 years ago. Slim chance you and I will ever see a decline in these costs.

In any case, long-term planning for "kid contingencies" is essential.

Financial Gifts

Another way of providing is to begin now with gifts of money, stocks and bonds. In accordance with the annual gift tax exclusion permitted under federal law, you and/or your spouse may each make gifts to your children of up to $10,000 a year per child without incurring a gift tax. If you or your spouse wish to make larger gifts, the unified estate and gift tax credit should be discussed with your accountant or attorney.

Under the Uniform Gifts to Minors Act, you may be the custodian of the funds or investments. You have the legal authority to hold and manage them on your children's behalf. If your children are under 14, any gains, dividends or interest over $1,000 will be taxed on your personal return. If over 14, they bear the responsibility of reporting the earned income on their own tax return. If they work part time and are under 14, the monies earned are taxable to them, not you the parent.

Informal Trust and Custodial Accounts

Both these types of accounts allow you to put money into a savings program for your children. With an informal trust account, you are considered the legal owner of the funds in the account, while the money in a custodial account legally belongs to your children.

U.S. Savings Bonds

All U.S. Savings Bonds are registered and printed with the Social Security numbers of their owners. If your children do not have Social Security numbers, you may purchase bonds imprinted with the word *gift*. These are then registered to your Social Security number. Do yourself a favor and obtain the forms requesting a number for each of your kids at your local Social Security office.

Stocks and Bonds

If you give gifts of stocks or bonds to children under 18 years of age, you must register the securities in your name or in the name of another adult as custodian for your children. If you use their Social Security number for the registration, earnings and gains will legally belong to them and will be taxable to their income if the earnings are less than $1,000 or they are over 14 years of age. Otherwise, any gain or income over $1,000 is taxed at your rate on your return.

INSURANCE FOR TWO OR MORE

Parenthood should also trigger a review of your insurance coverages. Inflation has increased the need for adequate protection against sudden loss of an individual's or a family's income, and life insurance is usually the primary source of cash following a death.

Your employer or your spouse's probably offers some life insurance coverage, but with children, you are almost certain to need more. Ideally, in the event of your death, your total coverage should be sufficient to replace your income for as long as your family requires it. Even if only one spouse is an income-producer, life insurance on both partners is a good idea. Too often, couples overlook the financial value of the nonworking parent, who is usually the homemaker as well as the primary care giver.

My advice is for a husband and wife to own life insurance policies on each other, each paying for the policies with funds that are seen clearly as separate property. The policies themselves (proceeds of separate property) are likewise separate property and can only be taxed in the owner's estate, not the insured's. That means the surviving spouse owns the policy outright. It is not subject to probate, and the money paid under the policy can be used to help pay any taxes without forcing a distressed sale of other properties or valuables.

The amount of insurance you need should be based on the property that may be taxable in case of death and on how many people depend upon you and the income you generate. If you don't have dependents, there's a high probability you don't need insurance at all. If you are receiving alimony or child support payments, you might consider taking out a policy on the life of the children's father. If he should die, the insurance policy would provide the money to replace the payments that are so essential, considering the costs of bringing up a child.

Term or Whole Life

There are basically two types of insurance: *term* and *whole life*. When you are talking with an insurance agent, he or she may offer what seems to be a vast array of types of insurance. There are lots of fancy names with different kinds of window dressing, but the basic format will be either term or whole life.

Term insurance is pure insurance. It offers a set amount of money to the beneficiary of the policy if the insured dies. You pay for one year's insurance at a time. In annual renewal term, the cost increases each year because you are one year closer to dying. Other types may keep the cost fixed for a few years, then hike it up. It's very similar to car and home insurance. If something catastrophic happens, you know the coverage is there.

We all grumble about the rising costs, but few of us really feel we can do without basic insurance on our home or cars. Term life insurance works in pretty much the same way. The older you get, the more costs increase. It is substantially lower in premium cost than whole life. The primary difference is that whole life has a savings account tied to it.

Let's say you had a policy for $100,000. Each year, you

pay the premium. As time passes, savings are accrued. At the time you bought the policy, the insurance company agreed to pay your beneficiary a total of $100,000 if you died. No more, no less. If the savings side amounts to $7,000, and you die, the insurance company returns the $7,000 to your beneficiary plus $93,000, totaling $100,000—not the savings plus the full amount of the insurance policy.

If you're under 45, term insurance is undoubtedly the least expensive and more reasonable choice. If you have children, I would advise you to purchase the amount of insurance necessary to provide an income that will take care of your dependents until they reach maturity or until your spouse or selected guardian can support them as you feel appropriate. In addition, when your attorney is reviewing your will and/or you have an update interview with your financial planner or accountant, you should estimate the taxes on your estate. If your estate will not have the cash to pay estate taxes, some type of insurance should be considered.

WHERE THERE'S A WILL, THERE'S A WAY

A final area of planning mandated by children is that of making a will. This kind of protection is every bit as important as the accumulation of your estate. It is, after all, your net worth, and even if you are just starting out with that "negative" net worth figure I mentioned earlier, there are intangible assets, such as yourself, your children, your personal belongings, which must be protected.

Who Will Care for the Children?

For starters, a will designates whom you want to take care

of your children. A 1987 front-page article in the *New York Times* remarked on how many parents *"neglect to name a guardian for their children"* in event of the parents' death. Perhaps their own death is not real to them, but it does seem incredible that parents will give minor children every advantage they're able to, but leave their entire future to chance by not making a will, or naming a guardian to look after the youngsters' welfare.

Financial Protection

Furthermore, you want to give your family some financial protection. Inheritance taxes alone can put your estate in debt. If your estate is less than $600,000, then taxes are irrelevant; there are none. Your children, family or groups you support are not irrelevant, however.

A will not only makes sure your estate goes to the heirs of your choice, it makes sure there's some estate left for them. Do you know, for instance, what the laws in your state are regarding inheritance? What happens if you have adopted children, stepchildren, errant children, aged parents, needy relatives or strong religious convictions? Will any of the money go to churches, missionaries or other Christian works?

These things must be spelled out. The average man spends more than 11,000 days of his life working to earn money. The average woman spends an untold number of days of her life working in, and outside the home, yet less than half of our men and even fewer women have wills.

If you do not have a will, the state will write one for you. And the state's will is predicated on standardized law, not on the needs, wants or desires of the participants. Even if your estate seems relatively insignificant, you would want monies and other items to go to those persons or institutions (i.e., the church) that you care about, not those designated by the state. The impact of dying intestate, without a will, is well put in this now classic column syndicated by Ann Landers.

DEAR READERS: If you want to do something nice for your family, get your affairs in order.

I came across this gem in *The Survivors,* a splendid magazine for widowed people. I obtained permission from the author, Judge Sam Harrod III, of Eureka, Illinois, to reprint it.

IF YOU DON'T HAVE A WILL
YOUR STATE HAS ONE FOR YOU

The Statutory "Will" of John Doe.

I, John Doe, make this my "will," by failing to have a will of my own choice prepared by my attorney.

1. I give one-half of all my property, both personal and real estate, to my CHILDREN, and the remaining one-half to my WIFE.

2. I appoint my WIFE as Guardian of my CHILDREN, if she survives me, but as a safeguard, I require that:

   a. my WIFE make written account every year to Probate Court, explaining how and why she spent money necessary for the proper care of our CHILDREN;

   b. my WIFE file a performance BOND, with sureties, to be approved by Probate Court, to guarantee she will properly handle our children's money;

   c. When our CHILDREN become adults, my WIFE

must file a complete, itemized, written account of everything she has done with our children's money;

d. when our SON and DAUGHTER become age 18, they can do whatever they please with their share of my estate;

e. no one, including my WIFE, shall have the right to question how our CHILDREN spend their shares;

3. If my WIFE does not survive me, or dies while any of our CHILDREN are minors, I do not nominate a Guardian of our CHILDREN, but hope relatives and friends may mutually agree on the one, and if they cannot agree, the Probate Court can appoint any Guardian it likes, including a stranger.

4. I do not appoint an Executor of my estate, and hope the Probate Court appoints someone I would approve.

5. If my WIFE remarries, the next husband:

a. shall receive one-third of all my WIFE'S property;

b. need not spend any of his share on our CHILDREN, even if they need support, and

c. can give his share to anyone he chooses, without giving a penny to our CHILDREN.

6. I do not care whether there are ways to lower my death taxes, and know as much as possible will go to the Government, instead of my WIFE and our CHILDREN. In witness whereof, I have completely failed to make a different will of my own choice with the advice of my attorney, because I really did not care to go to all that bother, and I adopt this, by default, as my "will."

(no signature required)[1]

Let the Experts Do It!

Your will should be prepared by a qualified tax or estate-planning attorney. Even if you feel you have sorted out all

---

By modeling your own values and demonstrating the fundamentals of financial responsibility, you can give your children an early understanding of both the importance and techniques of financial stewardship.

---

your holdings and specified, in a letter of intent, who gets what belongings, an expert is necessary for three reasons. First, the tax laws that deal with estate and trusts keep changing. Unless you are in the legal profession, it is highly unlikely you are going to be up-to-date on the current laws. Second, there are often inaccuracies in your writing, which could actually change your intent, and third, you may have forgotten something of value that should have been protected.

Review Again and Again

Once your will has been written, review it every three years or so, or whenever there is another tax act. Both state and federal laws keep changing; your family may have added children, grandchildren or in-laws that you want to include, or *exclude*; you may have accumulated or divested various pieces of property. All these should be stated in your will. It all may seem tedious, but once done it's done, and you can sleep better at night. "Wise men are praised for their wisdom; fools are despised for their folly" (Prov. 14:24). And so be it with women.

Pass Your Savvy On

Thus, money and kids go together. We have seen how children make money management even more important. But there is another aspect to responsible parenting: kids and money. As a woman, and now as a financially savvy woman, you are in an enviable and unique position to pass along valuable insights and concepts. By modeling your own values and demonstrating the fundamentals of financial responsibility, you can give your children an early understanding of both the importance and techniques of financial stewardship.

These are the seeds you sow for the future:

> Teach a child to choose the right path, and when he is older he will remain upon it (Prov. 22:6).
>
> Don't keep on scolding and nagging your children . . . . Bring them up with the loving discipline the Lord himself approves, with suggestions and godly advice (Eph. 6:4).
>
> My son, observe the commandment of your father, and do not forsake the teaching of your mother (Prov. 6:20, *NASB*).

It is noteworthy that in this last Bible verse, even Solomon, in the tenth century B.C., made reference to the different approach of men and of women. A man may tell a child what to do, but a woman is more likely to teach, show and guide him.

TODAY'S CHALLENGE

A mother's challenge, then, is to prepare her children to

live in the world as it really is, to accept money as the basis of our economy's barter system and to learn at home that industry and responsibility bring rewards, while laziness and irresponsibility bring difficulties. This, I might add, is a challenge all parents can respond to, not just women, whether it is through the family or through church, scouting or school groups.

Teach Them Young

But just how do you go about teaching children about budgeting, saving and thoughtful spending? In the early days, you begin by playing counting and number games. Letting children handle and count coins familiarizes them with money and helps them learn the value of the various coins and bills. Taking young children shopping also helps, but *taking* them is not enough—let them actually shop with you. You can let them make their own purchases, such as coloring books, stickers or food snack items. It is never too early to show children toys that costs $1 and two others that cost 50¢ each. Let them decide if they want the higher priced, presumably better item, or two less costly toys.

What About Allowances?

The pros and cons of regular allowances are often debated, but I think the positive values far outweigh the negative. An allowance gives school-age children practice in handling money. Without the discipline of an allowance, children will find it harder to make decisions such as, "Shall I buy three candy bars today or spread them out over the week?" "Shall I spend this money on stickers or put some in my piggy bank?"

It's Really a Matter of Choice

Decision making begins early. It's important that children make these decisions, not you, for there is no inherent right or wrong decision. It is simply a matter of making choices about money that children must live with. Three candy bars taste good on Monday, but on Tuesday does that decision still seem acceptable? Money management is, after all, a matter of value judgments rather than absolute right or wrong decisions. This approach is consistently reflected in *Penny Power* magazine, a monthly publication from Consumer Reports, aimed at helping young people understand, consider and evaluate how money should best be spent (or saved). One issue probed into allowances: when kids got them, how those without them managed, and even included a survey on how kids spend their money. The magazine does not tell a child what his or her decision should be; it only gives information and methods to arrive at one.

What Kind of Guide Are You?

Help your kids by devising a simple method of keeping track of what they spend each day, what they spend it on, and how much is left over at the end of the week. Use something like the budget found on the next page used by my niece Crissy.

This is the first step in establishing a simple budget, and it's one way you can begin a lifelong habit of planned spending. Like adults, children have fixed and flexible expenses.

At age 6, Crissy's allowance should be "walking around" money to be spent on whatever she wishes. By

CRISSY'S BUDGET

Month _____   Week _____

Money Received	Sat.	Sun.	Mon.	Tues.	Wed.	Thurs.	Fri.
Allowance	___	___	___	___	___	___	___
Odd Jobs	___	___	___	___	___	___	___
Gifts	___	___	___	___	___	___	___
Other _____	___	___	___	___	___	___	___
Total	___	___	___	___	___	___	___

Money Spent	Sat.	Sun.	Mon.	Tues.	Wed.	Thurs.	Fri.
Candy	___	___	___	___	___	___	___
Toys/Games	___	___	___	___	___	___	___
Gave to Friend	___	___	___	___	___	___	___
Pets	___	___	___	___	___	___	___
Clothes	___	___	___	___	___	___	___
Church	___	___	___	___	___	___	___
Savings	___	___	___	___	___	___	___
Snacks	___	___	___	___	___	___	___
Movies	___	___	___	___	___	___	___
Other _____	___	___	___	___	___	___	___
Total	___	___	___	___	___	___	___

Total Money Received $ _____

Total Money Spent $ _____

Over/Under $ _____

age 9 or 10, she should be able to compare her expenses to the size of her income (allowance, special jobs, baby-sitting) and develop some idea of spending priorities. By age 13, she should be able to break her allowance into three parts: spending money, fixed expenses (lunch or school supplies) and savings. If she loses money, which happens fairly often, don't replace it except for what is needed to cover the necessities she normally pays for.

Let children observe how you plan family purchases, from bringing a shopping list to the grocery store to setting aside money regularly for such major expenses as vacations. Observing the family budget will help them relate more easily to their own budget.

Families should talk about money openly. Did your parents share with you? Most likely not. And it's important that parents and children agree on the size of the allowance.

One last word on allowances. Be realistic. It should not be so small that it's a source of constant frustration, nor so large that he or she never has to make responsible choices.

Every Little Bit Counts

If your son or daughter doesn't have a bank savings account by age 13, a visit to the bank is in order. Although policies vary, most financial institutions will accept accounts for children who can sign their names legibly, and many will waive the minimum deposit requirements for opening an account if the saver is under 18.

One word of caution here. Some banks and savings and loans have a minimum service charge. Try to avoid them, as this fee could exceed the amount of interest earned, and savings could become a disincentive. You, or the new account representative, should explain the advantages of security in savings and extra earnings in the form of interest, as well as the forms and procedures for savings deposits and withdrawals.

Kids and Checking Accounts

A checking account for teenagers can also be useful, but this is a lot harder to implement. Most banks still require that checking account customers be at least 18 years old. Some still won't even consider joint accounts with the parents. Eventually, those will go the way of the dinosaur. In the meanwhile, it's worth the effort to search for a bank that will accommodate teenagers; if your child is willing, the lessons inherent in a checking account are numerous.

ABA Offers Classes for Kids

Even the American Bankers Association (ABA) recognizes the value of teenage education, for it inaugurated a personal economics program back in 1984, which now extends through 20 states and reaches over 775,000 teens. The program goes into every high school in a county for one week a year, one hour a day, and holds classes on how to balance a checkbook, use consumer credit and understand various bank services.

Kids Can Bank on It

However, it was not until the summer of 1987 that any practical application was made of this belief. Now there is The Young Americans Bank in Denver, Colorado, estab-

lished through the vision of Bill Daniels. With completion
of a survey in 1984, he found that, by 1990, 29 percent of
the U.S. population will be 18 or younger, teenagers
spend approximately $50 billion a year, and teens save
$9.3 billion annually

The Kids Bank is for young people between the ages

---

*Buying on credit is not about to disappear. So
it's increasingly important for your kids to
understand the rights and responsibilities that
go along with it.*

---

of 10 and 22. It offers checking accounts, personal loans
and business loans. Equally important, it is providing an
education: how to negotiate a loan, sign a check, manage a
savings account. Daniels thinks lack of training is the chief
cause of poor money management in America today; it
leads to budget problems, heavy reliance on credit cards
and ignorance as to the value of money market and stock
market mutual funds.

Teens and Budgets

During high school, teenagers should be able to budget for
a month at a time, or even for each quarter. A seasonal
clothes budget or a special trip, in addition to the allowance, is a good way to teach this kind of longer-range
budgeting.

Credit Shopping

It is also in the teen years that kids should be introduced to credit shopping. Buying on credit is not about to disappear. So it's increasingly important for your kids to understand the rights and responsibilities that go along with it. My girls are on their own now. But while in their teens, there were two important things I did.

Giving Teens Credit

First I put them on one of my MasterCard accounts, where each card user's name appeared individually and each was given a credit card. My job was to monitor them closely, and if they made any charges, to make sure that each paid her share of the bill. By adding their names to the account, they would establish their own credit file, which was my primary objective. Every time a payment was made, even if I had made it, they also got credit. The secondary objective was to familiarize them with money management. When something was purchased, it had to be paid for—"Those who play, have got to pay." In our house, that particular MasterCard was known as the "kids' account," and the adults did not use it.

Both girls are close in age but during their teen years, their sense of responsibility showed a broad gap. Sheryl abused her privilege by overcharging beyond her stated limit, resulting in the card immediately being taken away. Of course, as a parent, I had to make good the funds that were charged. If I did not, then I would have jeopardized her sister, who had been meeting her obligations by paying her charges when each bill arrived.

The second thing I did was introduce each to my banker when it was time to buy her first car. We went through the whole pretense of making a loan application. Of course, I had to guarantee the transaction, with my

name being added to the documents after they had completed them. As far as the girls were concerned, the loan
was in their name and there was an obligation to make the
monthly payment. If it wasn't paid, the bank would take
the car back.

As payments were made, the bank reported the transaction on the appropriate credit report. These two inci-
dents significantly increased my children's awareness of
what credit and money were all about. When Shelley
turned 18, she actually received an invitation to get her
own Visa card, which meant she no longer used the kids'
MasterCard. That was one of my goals for each of my
girls—to be able at some point to begin their credit lives
on the right foot.

As each daughter turned 18, the bank released me as
guarantor on the remaining loan balances, if any. During
the entire period, loan payments were made from their
checking accounts, never mine. There were some rough
spots—like the fact their checkbooks never balanced in
the beginning—but they learned. One time, the only solution was to close the account and open a new one—just to
know exactly what the beginning balance was. But that
was OK. That was part of the learning process.

SUMMING UP

Teaching youngsters about money in the formative years
can promote their intellectual development. It also helps
adults rethink the basics of money's value and the importance of making it grow. Children need to understand that
within today's society we seldom receive anything for
free. We work for what we receive. But if we work, we
have a right to expect to benefit.

If children function as responsible, cooperative, giving family members, if they understand and accept the "game rules," they should participate in the benefits. First Corinthians 9:10 shares, "Those who do the plowing and threshing should expect some share of the harvest."

Gifts of knowledge, understanding and self-discipline can have their own rewards for you as a mother and parent. "Correct your son, and he will give you comfort; he will also delight your soul" (Prov. 29:17, *NASB*).

NOTE
1. Reprinted from the *Peninsula Times Tribune* and used by permission of Ann Landers and the *Los Angeles Times* Syndicate.

CHAPTER EIGHT

Cash—Where to Park It

With this chapter we are beginning to examine your cash options—which of the various investment vehicles will be best for you, what the strengths and weaknesses of each might be and how each might fit into your financial plan.

The most obvious, and probably most familiar, option is the bank. The parable of the talents, as retold by Luke, takes on special significance here, for it introduces the concept that cash money, at the very least, should be in the bank:

> But the third man brought back only the money he had started with. "I've kept it safe," he said, "because I was afraid (you would demand my profits), for you are a hard man to deal with, taking what isn't yours and even confiscating the crops that others plant." "You vile and wicked slave," the king roared. "Hard, am I?

That's exactly how I'll be toward you! If you knew so much about me and how tough I am, then why didn't you deposit the money in the bank so that I could at least get some interest on it?" (Luke 19:20-23).

CASH IS KING

All of us need some ready cash, some liquid or accessible money. I recommend three to six months of after-tax income as a liquid reserve. Instant access means protection against the unexpected: the forgotten bill, the tax supplement, a medical emergency, or perhaps even a really exciting investment opportunity. When you look for liquid-

---

You want your cash to at least hold its own, as inflation tries to eat away at it.

---

ity, look for a guaranteed principal, where there is no likelihood of change in value. The key here is to look for the ability to receive the full market value of invested cash within seven working days. Thus some liquidity generally means protection against a loss of capital in the face of rapidly changing interest rates. It also works in times of inflation, when the cost of almost everything increases. You want your cash to at least hold its own, as inflation tries to eat away at it. But rampant inflation almost always heralds recession, and recession brings bargains both in investments and in personal purchases. Cycles are a common phenomenon in the money game, yet most of us forget how trends recur every few years.

Passbook Savings

A passbook savings account is the most common cash depository. This can be obtained from any financial institution with a minimum earned interest ranging from 4-½ percent and up. Banks and credit unions offer numerous variations on the traditional passbook savings, such as the computerized "statement savings," NOW accounts (standing for "negotiated order of withdrawal," referring, in banker's jargon, to a checking account that pays interest) and superNOW accounts with higher interest for guaranteed minimum deposits.

Pay attention to the fine print in all of these accounts, for bank fees, variable interest rates and taxable status of the interest will all affect the value of your savings. And even a clean 7-½ percent interest will not keep up with a 10 percent inflation rate. As with most decisions in the financial world, it's important to know all the facts, and to look at the whole picture. "Only a simpleton believes what he is told! A prudent man checks to see where he is going" (Prov. 14:15).

Committed Funds

One alternative to cash savings is a certificate of deposit (CD) or a time deposit. For amounts over $1,000, you can earn higher interest rates if you agree to commit your money for a period ranging from 30 days to 10 years. It takes a substantial amount of money and a long commitment period to get the highest rate. If you are thinking of a CD, it's important to shop around. Rates on CDs of any maturity can vary by as much as 2 percentage points from bank to bank, city to city and state to state.

There are also various marketing devices for CDs that range from frequent compounding to "zero coupon" discounting to variable interest rates to "split-rate," "expendable" or "convertible-term" CDs. Many of these variations are simply gimmicks. For any of them, you still need to look at the bottom-line yield.

You also need to look at the major drawbacks of CDs. Although they do offer immediate liquidity, you pay for that privilege. Do you recall the required advertising tag line, "Federal law requires substantial penalties for early withdrawal"? Banks are obliged to charge a penalty should you withdraw your funds before a certificate matures. These penalities are, indeed, substantial—the loss of up to six months' interest—while the remaining interest reverts to what a standard passbook would have paid during the same period. In other words, if you wish to receive the advertised high interest rate, your money isn't really liquid at all.

If you've already bought certificates and find you need immediate cash, calculate the amount of money you will lose from the penalty if you withdraw and compare it to the cost of a loan for the remainder of the period during which your cash is committed. It's quite possible it would make more sense to take out a loan to satisfy your cash needs and let the certificate come to maturity. The higher interest you will earn from the matured certificate may more than cover the interest charged on the loan. (Most banks will lend up to 90 percent of the face value of a deposit certificate.)

The bottom line? Before tying up any funds, ask how much money you will get at the end of the proposed period. Then compare.

Treasuries Offer Safety

If you have at least $10,000 to "park," treasury bills are a possibility. A treasury bill is technically a loan to the government, a loan that Uncle Sam guarantees to repay with interest in one year or less. Although they are issued in three maturities (91 days, six months, one year), they are negotiable. That is, they may be freely bought and sold after the government issues them. Thus it's possible to

---

Because of the flexibility that large cash assets afford them, money market funds pay top interest rates.

---

buy a T-bill due to be repaid by the Treasury in any week of the year. Like other interest income, interest on T-bills is taxed by the IRS. But it is free of state and local tax, which is no small bonus in high-tax states like New York, California, Wisconsin, Massachusetts and Minnesota. If you live in a state where there's no income tax, you lose a little of the tax benefit, but that's all.

More Liquid Assets

Another depository for liquid dollars is a money market fund. Money market funds were conceived in the 1970s to help small investors earn the highest interest rate available to those who had large sums of money for CDs, T-bills, commercial paper and the like. They are basically mutual funds that purchase only money instruments. They are not guaranteed by any federal agency, but the mutual fund companies that manage money market funds are regulated by the Securities and Exchange Commission.

Most money market funds allow you to write checks against your balance, some requiring a specified minimum amount, others none. You may make additional contributions to your fund, depending upon the stated minimum deposit. Although you do not have access to your funds in person (that is, there is no retail outlet such as a bank office), you can retrieve your money on a daily basis without penalty. Because of the flexibility that large cash assets afford them, money market funds pay top interest rates. There is a management fee involved, but it is relatively low compared to the interest and total liquidity offered. In this case, liquidity means you can get your money tomorrow, no need to wait seven days.

The idea of money market funds hit banks and savings and loan institutions hard. They responded by offering money market certificates, similar to money market funds except their interest was not compounded, they offered no check-writing privileges and the minimum outlay was $10,000. Management fees were eliminated, but there was a penalty for pulling out of the certificate before it matured. Today, some accounts have restraints, while others parallel the various options the money market funds offer.

Other Places to Stash Cash

There are other choices for "parking your cash," such as the cash value of life insurance, second trust deeds or annuities. These will be discussed in detail in later chapters. Of the above options, the money market funds are the most viable outlet for the small-to-medium investor looking for a good place to stash some cash. In 1982 alone,

there was more than $200 billion in over 160 different
money market funds. With that much money, you would
think everybody would know about them, but even today
only about 80 percent of the American population is really
aware what money funds are and what they can do.

You can obtain a prospectus or offering memorandum
from the funds by contacting them directly. Most companies advertise regularly in the business sections of your
local papers, as well as in the *Wall Street Journal.* Many
have toll-free 800 numbers you can call directly to request
a prospectus explaining goals, limitations and rules of the
fund.

Any cash should be earning more money for you. Period. Your job is to seek out the alternatives and then place
your funds so they can continue to grow. Each and every
day counts for each and every dollar.

CHAPTER NINE

The Ins and Outs of the Stock Market

Sooner or later, every investor will probably put some money in the stock market—even though many think of it as a dangerous jungle. They may be right! But, investing in stocks of sturdy, growing businesses is one way to help your dollars keep up with or even ahead of recurring inflation. The stock market to some is the symbol of our economic system. It is accessible and, in a sense, it seems downright patriotic to invest in the strength and fortitude of individual American businesses.

The stock market is a vehicle for growth—especially for the novice or small investor. It can, in fact, foster the kind of growth encouraged in 2 Corinthians 9;10: "For God, who gives seed to the farmer to plant, and later on, good crops to harvest and eat, will give you more and more seed to plant and will make it grow so that you can give away more and more fruit from your harvest."

Now, while it is true the stock market can be a lucrative investment opportunity, it can also be a bizarre and ephemeral circus, susceptible to whims and emotions: a

Las Vegas gambling hall with dozens of glittering games of chance. To invest in the stock market, you must know both the risks and the remedies.

TAKING THE PLUNGE

An understanding of the market is basic to our understanding of our underlying money management system. Also, it happens to be a place where smarts, common sense and sometimes a little luck can really pay off.

First of all, what is the stock market? Basically, it's where you buy ownership rights in an incorporated business. You are not lending money, you are actually buying part of the company. You have a claim on profits and, technically, a say in management and policy. Rarely, however, do stockholders exercise these rights. Most are realistic enough to see their role as passive. That is unless you are a major shareholder or attempting to take over the company à la T. Boone Pickins, the reknowned business takeover genius.

The value of a stock changes constantly. Basically, what it's worth is whatever someone else will pay for it. And that's determined at the stock exchange, a vast array of markets for stocks and bonds, where they are bought and sold by authorized agents via a stockbroker.

The business of the stock market is conducted on two major national exchanges: The New York Stock Exchange (NYSE) and the American Stock Exchange (AMEX). The NYSE has slightly stricter standards for the companies they list, but both require proven earnings records and demonstrated financial stability.

There is also an Over-the-Counter (OTC) market with countless securities not listed on an exchange, but ones that are traded among brokers over the phone with varying degrees of activity. Over-the-Counter stocks are not necessarily riskier. It's just that many well-known companies have chosen to stay listed merely in the Over-the-Counter market verses trading on the New York Stock Exchange, the American Stock Exchange or many of the other exchanges of a much smaller degree, such as the Midwest Stock Exchange or the Pacific Coast Stock Exchange. Don't feel you have to shy away from a stock just because it's not listed on the "Big Board."

GROWTH VS. INCOME

There are two primary types of stock: growth stocks and income stocks. A growth company often pays little, if any, cash dividends, because it tends to be a newer or smaller company and is likely to plow a large share of its earnings back into the company—for research and development or further growth and expansion. Classic examples are companies in the technology field. A substantial part of their market price represents prospects for the future, rather than past performance. The value of the stock itself is expected to rise substantially over the coming years, so you can gain in value without having to pay taxes before you sell.

Growth stocks could be useful for younger couples who don't need cash income immediately, gifts for children to be held on a long-term basis or stockholders with high incomes who would be forced to give the IRS a chunk of any dividends.

High-yield, or income, stocks are just that—stocks that distribute a large portion of the profits to stockholders in the form of a cash dividend. Utility stocks fit in here.

Somewhere in the middle of these two are what are known as blue chip stocks. These are supposedly conservative, proven stocks, which offer some growth, a respectable dividend and, hopefully, peace of mind. Many think of AT&T, IBM, Proctor & Gamble and Johnson & Johnson as classic examples of blue chip stocks.

A daily check of the Dow Jones listings can help you keep abreast of the overall thrust of the market.

Throughout this chapter, the concept of "what goes up will come down" is reinforced. The above companies are all well-known and managed. Their stock values also oscillate widely.

THE DOW JONES INDUSTRIAL AVERAGES

Usually I do not recommend daily checking on single stocks, but a daily check of the Dow Jones listings can help you keep abreast of the overall thrust of the market. Exact, it is not. It consists of only 30 stocks and is not updated on an ongoing basis to parallel the various growth industries as they emerge.

In 1987, two new listings were brought on—Coca-Cola and Boeing—both major companies and both more in tune to today's environment. The companies they replaced were older—Owens-Illinois and Inco. Owens-Illinois is being taken private. That is, its stock can no longer be bought on the open market. Inco is a nickel and copper producer—an issue that today's investor doesn't appear to have much interest in.

By scanning these quotations, you can get a good idea of what went on the day before and try to spot patterns correlating with other news items that may influence the market. Here's an example of a quotation for Helene Curtis from the *Wall Street Journal* and an explanation of how to read it:

Sample Stock Quotation in the *Wall Street Journal* for activity March 16, 1987

(1) 52 Weeks		(2)	(3)	(4)	(5)	(6)	(7)	(8)	(9)	(10)
				%	P.E.	(100)				Net
High	Low	Stock	Div.	Yld.	Ratio	Sales	High	Low	Close	Change
38¼	22⅝	HelneC	.30e	.9	12	21	35½	35	35	—¾

1. In the last 52 weeks the stock has traded as high as 38-¼ per share and as low as 22-⅝ per share.
2. The name of the company or stock—note it is abbreviated.
3. The amount of the dividend paid per share per year. *"e"* means that 30¢ per share was paid the preceding year and has not been declared for the current year.
4. The percentage return of the dividend in relation to the current price per share.
5. Represents the price of a share divided by earnings per share for a 12-month period. In our illustration, Helene Curtis is selling for $35 per share and the stated P.E. ratio is 12. If you divide 35 by 12, the result is approximately $2.92, which represents earnings for the past 52 weeks.
6. Sales are reported in 100s, so multiply 21 by 100, arriving at 2,100 shares traded on March 16, 1987.
7. Stock traded as high as 35-½ per share during the day.

8. Stock traded as low as 35 during the day.
9. Stock closed at 35 per share.
10. Stock closed ¾ of a point below the preceding day.

CHOOSING A STOCK

You have undoubtedly heard stories of how choosing stocks as if you were playing darts often produces better results than if you consulted with the most reputable stockbroker. In truth, there does seem to be some luck involved, but so are logic and rationale. Over the years I have become convinced there are plenty of areas where any novice investor, willing to do *some* serious homework, can out-perform the vast majority of professionals. This conviction is based on the results of innumerable weekend seminars I have given across the country to uninformed, supposedly unsophisticated women. Consider this one example.

A weekend class had been scheduled at the University of California at Santa Cruz. Approximately 40 women attended. Those who were from out of the immediate area stayed overnight in the dorms. A few days before the classes began, *Business Week* magazine published an article covering the fast food industry. The first day of class I presented the market and its various options and gave some simple rules for evaluating the information available to every investor considering a stock purchase. I'm a firm believer the last thing any of us really needs to be successful is inside information.

I showed this group how to determine book values, evaluate percentages, compare the market and book-value increases, even showed them how simple it was to determine the price earnings ratio.

Of the companies presented, I chose several that had *Value Line* surveys and presented them in the afternoon. *Value Line* is one of the top rated advisories and is available at no cost at most brokerage houses and libraries, or to individuals for an annual fee. Samples will be used as illustrations later in this chapter. I find them an invaluable tool.

Women were asked to evaluate each of the stocks and pick the one that seemed to have the best chance of increasing in value, using the standard I had described. What was that standard? Nothing very complicated, merely going back over the last five years to determine what percentage increases or decreases had occurred from year to year in earnings per share, book values, price earnings ratios, capital expenditures, sales per share, profit margin and other areas I had pointed out. This assignment kept class members busy all evening.

The following morning they returned to class and presented their choices. Almost all had been able to select the stock that seemed most appealing. That stock, 11 years ago, was all but unknown. Today its shares are owned all over the world by major institutions, as well as women like you and me. In the year after the class the stock had increased significantly in price. It showed itself to be aggressive and forward-looking. The market appreciated the vision of its management. It was no surprise to the stock market neophytes who met that weekend in Santa Cruz. The stock? Wendy's Old Fashioned Hamburgers.

What I taught these women was quite simple. I showed them some of the key essentials to look for in a stock, but I also showed them how to apply common sense in evaluating a possible stock purchase.

In earlier chapters, I wrote about how to look for

trends as a consumer and how to use that knowledge in pursuit of stocks. Now it's time to reinforce it, and remember that every major journey must have its beginning. It usually isn't sufficient a stock or a group of companies be riding a wave. Remember, all waves crash, and when a stock climbs quickly, oftentimes it's the first to fall, especially when there is a vogue or fad involved.

Always, *always* keep in mind the phenomenal success of Pet Rocks. They sold like hotcakes one Christmas. Another item, the Cabbage Patch doll, was the hottest Christmas item a couple of years ago. The dolls were going for $100 to $200. Just a year later, the price of those dolls dropped significantly, as did the earnings per share of the parent company, Coleco. Was this a trend? Absolutely not, closer to a fad.

The only times fortunes and empires are built on fads are when those who trade or invest in them can get out before everyone else gets in.

If you sight something you feel is involved in a trend, determine the product's owner and the exchange on which their stock is traded, if it is. The next step is to tune in— learn to examine:

The Balance Sheet

Current assets of a company should outnumber liabilities by at least two to one. The greater the ratio in favor of assets, the better for the stockholder. Of course, there are exceptions to every rule. Companies in the high technology areas often require a higher ratio of assets because they expend so much effort in research and development. On the other hand, railroads, airlines and utilities often operate successfully with less than a two to one ratio.

Another ratio to look closely at is the quick ratio, or acid test. That's determined by taking all the current assets on the balance sheet and deducting inventory. The remaining number is then compared to current liabilities. The ratio you're looking for is one to one. Bankers look closely at this ratio. The reason? If inventory can't be sold, they want to make sure there's sufficient cash available to meet the ongoing payables and debt requirements of the company.

You need to think like the banker. There's nothing worse than yesterday's product you can never sell.

The Earnings Record

A company's earnings should either be consistent over the past several years or show continuing increase. There will always be peaks and valleys, especially if the overall economy goes through a whopping recession. A speculative investor, someone who is often going for an aggressive growth position looks for companies that have high ups and low downs, hoping to find and hit the right pattern. For you, as a first time investor, this strategy should be avoided like the plague.

The Dividend Record

If you're buying a stock for income purposes, make sure you research its dividend payments for the last 10 years. They need to have been paid consistently, with an increase per annum over that period. Don't give up on a stock that has one bad year. Companies often do. Again, if you see a downturn, look at what happened to the overall economy during that specific time.

The Price Earnings Ratio

Computing the Price Earnings (PE) ratio is easily done by dividing the current market price of a stock by the last known earnings per share. This figure is given in most stock advisories, and certainly in your daily newspaper. If a stock sells at $40 a share and has earnings of $5 a share, then its price earnings ratio is 8—40 divided by 5. Normally, the higher the PE ratio, the more risk involved.

Pricing Reality

Stocks are usually priced for a reason—good or poor management, growth possibilities, outside influences like government regulation, inconsistency in marketing, pricing and policy. There are a whole variety of reasons. Your job is to probe in and find out what some of those reasons may be.

Finally, when you have these numbers, it's critical for you to apply your common sense and overall perception of what the trends currently are and what they may be in the future. Look at a company's line of products in relationship to consumer tastes and preferences. Keep in mind any information you've collected from outside sources, such as magazines or newspapers, can influence the price of the stock.

Wonder of Wonders

When I dictated the first draft of this chapter in the winter of 1987 I had just read an article from the *Wall Street Journal*. That article talked about a company by the name of World of Wonders. It went on to share facts about its new product line.

Who is World of Wonders? In 1985, they brought us Teddy Ruxpin, the first talking bear who told stories. When this not too cuddly animal was introduced, World of Wonders' stock rocketed. In the first day of trading, it almost doubled in price per share. That was in 1986. Later in the year, an article circulated in a major business magazine that the company was really a one product firm and predicted that it could not sustain its phenomenal growth. The market took that to heart and its stock price plummeted immediately. Within two weeks, another announcement came from the company revealing its new line for the following Christmas: a significant expansion on the initial single product of Teddy Ruxpin. The market kneejerked again and the price of the stocks shot up.

This latest article told of the company's expansion into the educational field—a natural market. If the children grow up with Teddy Ruxpin, why not continue with related educational items at school? The stock reacted, reversed itself and increased in value.

The story continues. In December 1987, Worlds of Wonder filed for bankruptcy. The educational line hadn't taken off as projected and Christmas sales were weak. The stock plummeted again. At this point, who knows what the next chapter will be.

Comparison Shopping

When you're considering a company for investment purposes, it makes sense to compare that company with others in the same field. Determine what its specific averages are, its increases and decreases in several areas, such as earnings per share, net worth, dividends, revenues per share, capital spending per share, operating profit and working capital.

Much of this information can be found in the resource I mentioned earlier, the *Value Line Survey.* On page 146 and 147 is a chart of a company that may be very familiar to you, Helene Curtis. Note the key areas I have highlighted for you:

1. This chart illustrates that Helene Curtis has fluctuated in price, beginning in 1970, with a trading range less than $1 per share, to a high of $38-3/8 per share. As you can see, the stock has had some price swings, but not as wide ranging as that of Neutrogena, which you'll read about in subsequent pages.

   If you had purchased this stock in mid-1975, you'll note there was not much action in the price through 1980. Certainly this is one you would not have made your fortune on. But on the other hand, because of the minimal price movement, it is not one in which you would have lost your grocery money either.

   The year 1981 showed a slight movement in the stock on the upside, then a decline, then a significant increase from $6 a share to $36 a share within a three-year period—a handsome increase for those who were patient.

   Helene Curtis's stock is owned by many institutions, including mutual funds such as the Templeton Group.

2. Note that Helene Curtis paid a 100 percent dividend on its shares in 1984.

3. Helene Curtis had a two-for-one stock split—for every share you had, you now have double that number.

4. Be aware of the timeliness and safety rankings. Both

these are based on a one-to-five scale, with one being the best. Helene Curtis is ranked two in timeliness. That means it's above average and its market value is increasing ahead of the overall Dow Jones Average. It's safety is four. This is based on the financial position of the company as well as the oscillation of the stock.

5. Take projections with a grain of salt.
6. The actual financial reports are important. Note the increased sales per share, earning per share, book value per share, capital spending (if a company is planning any growth, there should always be funds allocated for capital spending), average annual PE ratio, and net profit margins.
7. If you desire income from your investments, note the kind of dividends per share. Helene Curtis did not begin paying dividends until 1986. Therefore, if you need income, this is not a stock that will meet your criteria. The amount it pays is minimal and it does not have a track record over a span of time in dividend payments for you to rely on.
8. The center section is important. It tells who the company is, what their major products are, who the CEO (Chief Executive Officer) is, the company location and address, and phone number. It often shares a percentage split of where revenues per major product lines are received. An interesting side note: When you address complaint letters to the CEO, action usually results.
9. Major information is noted, as well as changes in directions of the company and how the investment community feels or projects. For those of you who are interested in career changes or job repositioning,

HELENE CURTIS NYSE-HC

RECENT PRICE	23	P/E RATIO	16.3	(Trailing:12.7 Median:8.5)	RELATIVE P/E RATIO	1.29	DIV'D YLD	0.9%	VALUE LINE	820

TIMELINESS 3 (Relative Price Perform- ance Next 12 Mos.) Average

SAFETY 3 Average (Scale: 1 Highest to 5 Lowest)

BETA 1.15 (1.00 = Market)

1992-94 PROJECTIONS

	Price	Gain	Ann'l Total Return
High	50	(+115%)	22%
Low	30	(+30%)	6%

Insider Decisions

	J	J	A	S	O	N	D	J	F
to Buy	0	0	0	0	0	0	0	0	0
Options	0	0	0	0	0	0	0	0	0
to Sell	1	2	1	2	1	0	0	0	0

Institutional Decisions

	2Q'89	3Q'89	4Q'89
to Buy	15	15	18
to Sell	13	6	13
Hld's(000)	3920	4152	4173

Percent shares traded: 12.0 / 8.0 / 4.0

8.0 x "Cash Flow" p sh

Relative Price Strength

Options: None

Target Price Range 1992 | 1993 | 1994 | 1995

	1974	1975	1976	1977	1978	1979	1980	1981	1982	1983	1984	1985	1986	1987	1988	1989	1990	1991	© VALUE LINE, INC.	92-94E
High	2.5					18.52	21.77	25.82	31.76	41.98	47.36	46.06	51.15	62.10	65.62	76.65	89.60			
Low	1.5																			
Sales per sh A	9.99	12.32	13.88	14.51	15.94		21.77	25.82	31.76	41.98	47.36	46.06	51.15	62.10	65.62	76.65	89.60			119.80
"Cash Flow" per sh	.31	.37	.43	.59	.42	.56	.90	.98	.87	1.85	.97	1.81	2.21	2.48	2.46	3.00	2.80			5.40
Earnings per sh B	.22	.26	.30	.45	.22	.31	.59	.63	.49	1.42	.37	1.22	1.40	1.47	1.72	1.81	1.65			3.65
Div'ds Decl'd per sh C	.11	.32	.32	.26	.31	.41	.74	1.39	.15	.15	.15	.15	.15	.15	.15	.18	.20			.55
Cap'l Spending per sh	.11							1.63	2.23		1.98	1.66	1.69	2.02	3.71	4.70	2.60			3.15
Book Value per sh E	2.20	2.57	2.99	3.45	3.72	4.13	4.75	5.31	5.60	6.79	7.10	8.59	9.90	11.28	13.75	15.10	16.65			23.95
Common Shs Outst'g E	8721	8.58	8.54	8.55	8.21	7.79	7.49	7.52	7.66	7.87	7.82	7.83	7.82	7.87	9.59	9.60	9.60			9.60
Avg Ann'l P/E Ratio	3.4	6.2	5.1	3.8	9.9	6.0	3.8	6.0	8.5	7.3	28.4	7.8	10.5	11.0	11.0	15.4	Bold figures are Value Line estimates			11.0
Relative P/E Ratio	.48	.65	.50	1.35	.87	.50	.73	.94	.62	.63	.71	.72	.91	1.18			.90			
Avg Ann'l Div'd Yield												1.0%	.9%	.8%	.6%					.9%

CAPITAL STRUCTURE as of 11/30/89
Total Debt $103.5 mill. Due in 5 Yrs $65.0 mill.
LT Debt $99.7 mill. LT Interest $10.0 mill.
Incl. $6.0 mill. capitalized leases.
(LT interest earned: 3.6x; total interest coverage: 3.5x) (41% of Cap'l)
Leases, Uncapitalized Annual rentals $4.3 mill.
Pension Liability $4.9 mill. in '88 vs. $5.5 mill. in '87

Pfd Stock None

Common Stock 9,624,951 shs. E (59% of Cap'l)
"Common": 6,082,177 shs. Class B: 3,542,774 shs.

	1980	1981	1982	1983	1984	1985	1986	1987	1988	1989	1990	1991		92-94E
Sales ($mill) A	163.1	194.3	243.2	330.4	370.3	360.8	400.1	488.9	629.2	736.0	860			1150
Operating Margin	7.8%	7.6%	5.2%	8.3%	3.1%	7.7%	7.9%	6.6%	6.0%	6.6%	5.8%			6.5%
Depreciation ($mill)	2.2	2.6	3.1	4.1	4.9	5.3	7.0	8.7	9.2	12.0	14.0			18.0
Net Profit ($mill)	4.5	4.8	3.6	10.4	2.7	8.9	10.3	10.8	14.4	16.8	13.0			34.0
Income Tax Rate	50.2%	52.1%	41.5%	48.2%	48.0%	48.0%	49.8%	45.5%	41.0%	42.2%	42.0%			42.0%
Net Profit Margin	2.8%	2.5%	1.5%	3.2%	.7%	2.5%	2.6%	2.2%	2.3%	2.3%	1.5%			3.0%
Working Cap'l ($mill)	31.6	37.9	38.7	41.6	46.7	45.9	49.0	53.4	87.3	120	160			265
Long-Term Debt ($mill)	10.8	25.7	27.5	32.9	46.5	29.9	28.9	32.4	50.8	110	145			215
Net Worth ($mill)	35.6	39.9	42.9	53.4	55.5	67.3	77.4	88.8	131.8	147	160			220
% Earned Total Cap'l	10.6%	9.2%	7.1%	13.7%	4.9%	11.1%	11.4%	10.5%	9.0%	8.0%	6.5%			10.0%
% Earned Net Worth	12.8%	11.9%	8.4%	19.5%	4.9%	13.3%	13.3%	12.2%	10.9%	11.5%	8.0%			15.0%
% Retained to Comm Eq	12.8%	11.9%	8.4%	19.5%	4.9%	13.3%	12.0%	11.1%	10.1%	10.5%	7.5%			12.5%
% All Div'ds to Net Prof							10%	9%	8%	10%	14%			10%

CURRENT POSITION ($MILL.)

	1987	1988	11/30/89
Cash Assets	3.2	3.4	7.1
Receivables	93.3	123.2	108.7
Inventory (LIFO)	56.3	84.2	105.2
Other	4.3	4.4	16.6
Current Assets	157.1	215.2	237.6
Accts Payable	40.9	51.2	55.8
Debt Due	6.6	13.6	3.8
Other	56.2	63.1	64.9
Current Liab.	103.7	127.9	124.5

ANNUAL RATES

of change (per sh)	Past 10 Yrs.	Past 5 Yrs.	Est'd '86-'88 to '92-'94
Sales	15.0%	12.5%	12.5%
"Cash Flow"	17.5%	14.0%	14.5%
Earnings	17.0%	12.5%	15.5%
Dividends	--	--	15.0%
Book Value	13.0%	14.5%	13.0%

QUARTERLY SALES ($ mill) A

Fiscal Year Begins	May 31	Aug.31	Nov.30	Feb.28	Full Fiscal Year
1986	86.8	104.2	97.0	113.9	400.1
1987	101.9	129.5	120.6	136.9	488.9
1988	137.8	157.2	163.6	170.6	629.2
1989	160.2	199.0	169.8	207.0	736.0
1990	195	220	210	235	860

EARNINGS PER SHARE A B

Fiscal Year Begins	May 31	Aug.31	Nov.30	Feb.28	Full Fiscal Year
1986	d.11	.27	.42	.82	1.40
1987	.02	d.20	.52	1.13 c	1.47
1988	.22	.65	.41	.44	1.72
1989	.24	.71	.28	.58	1.81
1990	.05	.50	.40	.50	1.45

QUARTERLY DIVIDENDS PAID C

Calendar	Mar.31	Jun.30	Sep.30	Dec.31	Full Year
1986	--	--	--	--	.08
1987	.075	--	--	--	.15
1988	.075	--	--	--	.15
1989	.075	--	--	--	.15
1990	.075	.05	--	--	.20

BUSINESS: Helene Curtis Industries, Inc. produces hair care items and other toiletries. Major brand names: *Suave*, popular-priced hair care and toiletry products; *Finesse* and *Salon Selectives*, premium-priced hair care lines; *Degree* antiperspirant (introduced in 1989). Professional division supplies hair care products to beauty salons. Protective Treatments subsidiary sold 10/85. Has manufacturing and warehouse facilities in Illinois and California. Advertising: 12% of sales. Foreign sales: 22% of total. '88 deprec. rate: 7.0%. Has 2,900 employees, 2,066 shareholders. Gidwitz Family Group owns 34% of stock and controls 74% of voting shares. Chairman: Gerald Gidwitz. President & C.E.O.: Ronald Gidwitz. Inc.: IL. Address: 325 North Wells Street, Chicago, IL 60610. Telephone: 312-661-0222.

A raft of new product activity will hurt Helene Curtis's earnings in fiscal 1990 (ends February 28, 1991). The company plans to spend $50 million to support its *Degree* antiperspirant rollout this year, which will cost about $5 million pretax. In addition, Helene Curtis is currently launching *Salon Selectives* in Japan and *Finesse* in West Germany. Although these two introductions will add an estimated $40 million to the top line in fiscal 1990, they probably will hurt pretax earnings by another $7 million to $10 million.

The core hair care lines are performing well, though. The *Salon Selectives* brand, introduced in 1987, is now a $150 million product line and seems poised to grow another 15%-20% in the current 12-month cycle. *Suave*, meanwhile, is benefiting from a 10% price reduction last year that enhanced its competitiveness in the price-value segment of consumer hair care. Its unit sales surged 20% in the fourth quarter of fiscal 1989, and we expect this momentum to continue for the next couple of quarters. The only laggard is the *Finesse* line, which is encountering increased competition from other premium-priced offerings. Nevertheless, we expect *Finesse* to maintain market share in the year ahead.

We estimate earnings will drop 20% this fiscal year. Costs relating to the new products will likely overwhelm any gains relating to Helene Curtis's steadily increasing operating and purchasing efficiencies. (The recent completion of a new distribution facility, for example, will generate $5 million in savings in fiscal 1990.) **This stock's merits will likely become more apparent over the 3- to 5-year haul.** To date, management has emphasized sales growth over profits in order to build the critical mass necessary to compete effectively against industry behemoths like Procter & Gamble. As company sales approach the $1 billion mark in the next few years, though, we think management will begin to focus on fattening margins. Assuming Helene regains the profitability it enjoyed in the mid-1980s, earnings gains should be explosive beyond fiscal 1990. If we're correct, these shares will be worthwhile performers to 1992-94. Patient investors should look for a buying opportunity around the $20-a-share mark.
Paul A. Graham, Jr.   *April 20, 1990*

Company's Financial Strength	B+
Stock's Price Stability	30
Price Growth Persistence	90
Earnings Predictability	45

(A) Fiscal yr. ends Feb. 28th of next calendar year. (B) Primary egs. Excl. discont. ops in '85, 57¢. Next egs. report due late June. Last quarterly dividend of 5¢ a share was initiated in November. Future div'd payment dates have yet to be determined. (D) Accounting principle for interim advertising & promotional expense was changed in '88. Restated '87 quarterly e.p.s.: 9¢, 76¢, 27¢, 35¢. (E) In millions, adj. for stock split and div'd. Common shares have dividend priority and 1 vote. Class B shares have 10 votes, are convertible into common shares.

13

this is an ideal section to read. Knowing about future products may put you one up in an interview.

10. Current position represents the last two years, as well as the current year with a break-out of assets and liabilities.
11. Represents the annual rates for the past five and ten years on percentage increases for sales, cash flow, earnings, dividends and book value. It often includes estimates in increases or decreases for the next period of time.
12. Current financial data on dividends paid, quarterly sales and earnings per share for the preceding four years, as well as estimates for the current year.
13. The company's financial strength is important. If you are conservative, then it makes sense to go with an *A* or better rating. If you are willing to take a little risk and look at companies that may be turn-around candidates or fairly new on the investment scene, then a rating of less than *A* may be perfectly alright.

Time to Probe

Now let's take a look at an investment in Helene Curtis. Let's say that you purchased 100 shares in 1980. The stock was selling for approximately $4 per share—an investment of $400 plus commission. For illustration purposes, I will ignore commissions.

Through 1980 and 1981, the stock appreciated, dropped somewhat in 1982 and then began to climb again through 1984 and has oscillated in price since that time. In 1984, a 100 percent dividend was paid increasing your holdings to 200 shares. In 1989 there was a two-for-one split. This means that your 200 shares now numbers 400.

In looking at the market value on April 20, 1990 at $23 a share, your overall holdings have appreciated from $400 to $9,200 or an $8,800 profit. In 1986, a 30 cents a share dividend was declared yielding $60 for your 200 shares and in 1989 with the two-for-one stock split, the dividend was adjusted to reflect the split (from 30 cents to 15 cents) and then increased to 18 cents a share. The total amount you will receive in dividends for your 400 shares is $72 a year.

In other words, during the 10 years of holding Helene Curtis stock, your money has increased 2,200 percent—not bad. But, could you have done better? Let's look at another company in the same health care/cosmetic related field, Neutrogena (see next page).

Coincidentally in the same year, 1980, 100 shares of Neutrogena could have been purchased for $4 per share (see number 1 on its Value Line). Prior to 1973, there was no public trading in the company. Prior to 1980, the price per share was so low that it falls off the chart. But note that it was growing in value via the earnings per share as well as gradual increase in sales per share (see number 2 on chart).

In 1981, the stock experienced a two-for-one split increasing your holding to 200 shares. In 1982, a 10 percent dividend was paid increasing your holdings to 220 shares. In 1984, a two-for-one split was again declared (see 3) increasing your holdings to 440 shares. In 1986, a three-for-two split was declared increasing your holdings to 660 shares (see 4) and repeated in 1987, shares increased to 1,485 and again in 1988 shares increased to 2,227 (see 5 and 6). A 25 percent stock dividend was declared in 1986 (see 7)—another 556 shares.

Neutrogena also paid dividends but began far earlier than Helene Curtis, an old established company. In the

NEUTROGENA OTC-NGNA

RECENT PRICE	23	
P/E RATIO	20.0	(Trailing: 23.0 / Median: 24.0)
RELATIVE P/E RATIO	1.59	
DIV'D YLD	1.0%	
VALUE LINE	821	

TIMELINESS 3 Average (Relative Price Performance Next 12 Mos.)
SAFETY 3 Average (Scale: 1 Highest to 5 Lowest)
BETA 1.00 (1.00 = Market)

1992-94 PROJECTIONS

	Price	Gain	Ann'l Total Return
High	50	(+115%)	22%
Low	35	(+50%)	12%

Insider Decisions
Institutional Decisions

| High: | 1.0 | 1.4 | ... |
| Low: | 0.6 | 0.9 | ... |

CAPITAL STRUCTURE as of 1/31/90
Total Debt None
Leases, Uncapitalized Annual rentals $.7 mill.
Pension Liability None in 89 vs. None in '88
Pfd Stock None

Options: None
© VALUE LINE, INC.

Per-share statistical array

	1974	1975	1976	1977	1978	1979	1980	1981	1982	1983	1984	1985	1986	1987	1988	1989	1990	1991	92-94E
Sales per sh A	.30	.38	.49	.69	.81		1.00	1.11	1.67	1.76	2.34	2.92	3.74	5.24	6.84	7.78	8.40		14.15
"Cash Flow" per sh B	.03	.04	.05	.07	.08		.08	.11	.16	.15	.20	.29	.37	.65	.98	1.14	1.35		2.25
Earnings per sh B	.03	.04	.05	.06	.07		.07	.09	.11	.12	.16	.23	.30	.55	.86	.99	1.15		2.00
Div'ds Decl'd per sh C	--	--	--	.01	.01		.01	.01	.01	.02	.03	.03	.04	.06	.11	.16	.20		.22
Cap'l Spending per sh C	.02	.01	.01	.02	.02		.05	.02	.04	.05	.11	.18	.14	.27	.62	.58	.50		.55
Book Value per sh D	.11	.14	.18	.21	.28	.33	.38	.46	.33	.40	.49	.73	1.03	1.48	2.25	3.00	4.00		8.70
Common Shs Outst'g E	27.32	27.32	28.99	27.71	29.19		29.37	29.55	23.43	29.51	25.28	25.48	25.68	25.80	26.15	26.11	26.35		26.50
Avg Ann'l P/E Ratio	6.5	6.0	7.3	12.0	8.5	9.8	16.1	22.2	20.4	22.4	28.1	39.8	30.0	31.0	23.6				21.0
Relative P/E Ratio	.91	.80	.93	1.57	1.42		2.14	2.70	2.25	2.09	2.28	2.70	2.56	2.57	1.78				1.75
Avg Ann'l Div'd Yield				1.1%	1.1%		.8%	.5%	.7%	.8%	.7%	.5%	.4%	.3%	.4%	.7%			.8%

Bold figures are Value Line estimates

Company financials

	1980	1981	1982	1983	1984	1985	1986	1987	1988	1989	1990	92-94E
Sales ($mill) A	29.4	32.9	39.2	45.5	59.2	74.5	96.0	135.1	178.9	203.2	205	375
Operating Margin	12.8%	15.4%	15.8%	14.6%	14.9%	17.2%	17.7%	21.4%	22.5%	22.5%	22.5%	25.0%
Depreciation ($mill)	.5	.6	.6	.6	.9	1.3	1.5	1.8	2.5	2.9	4.0	5.0
Net Profit ($mill)	2.0	2.7	3.1	3.2	4.2	6.2	8.1	14.9	23.0	26.8	32.0	55.0
Income Tax Rate	48.6%	49.5%	50.5%	48.2%	48.3%	47.4%	50.5%	47.3%	40.8%	40.0%	39.0%	41.0%
Net Profit Margin	6.8%	8.1%	7.8%	7.0%	7.1%	8.4%	8.5%	11.0%	12.9%	13.2%	13.6%	14.7%
Working Cap'l ($mill)	7.4	9.8	3.4	5.6	5.6	8.8	14.8	21.7	29.6	36.1	50.0	125
Long-Term Debt ($mill)	--	--	--	--	--	--	--	--	--	--	Nil	Nil
Net Worth ($mill)	11.3	13.7	7.6	10.4	12.3	18.5	26.4	38.1	58.9	78.4	105	220
% Earned Total Cap'l	17.7%	19.5%	40.2%	30.6%	34.5%	33.5%	30.8%	39.1%	39.1%	34.1%	30.5%	24.0%
% Earned Net Worth	17.7%	19.5%	40.2%	30.6%	34.5%	33.5%	30.8%	39.1%	39.1%	34.1%	30.5%	24.0%
% Retained to Comm Eq	15.4%	17.1%	26.2%	30.6%	29.4%	29.2%	26.6%	35.5%	34.2%	28.8%	24.0%	19.5%
% All Div'ds to Net Prof	13%	12%	83%	14%	15%	13%	13%	9%	13%	16%	17%	16%

Common Stock 26,280,575 shs. (100% of Cap'l)

CURRENT POSITION ($MILL.)	1988	1989	1/31/90
Cash Assets	21.8	35.7	15.6
Receivables	20.7	23.5	27.7
Inventory (FIFO)	16.1	17.4	19.8
Other	2.7	3.8	7.3
Current Assets	61.3	80.4	70.4
Accts Payable	10.8	14.9	11.1
Debt Due	--	--	--
Other	20.9	29.4	18.7
Current Liab.	31.7	44.3	29.8

ANNUAL RATES of change (per sh)	Past 10 Yrs.	Past 5 Yrs.	Est'd '87-'89 to '92-'94
Sales	25.5%	28.0%	16.5%
"Cash Flow"	30.0%	43.5%	20.0%
Earnings	31.0%	18.5%	24.0%
Dividends	34.5%	--	--
Book Value	23.5%	41.0%	31.0%

Fiscal Year Ends	QUARTERLY SALES ($ mill.) A Jan.31	Apr.30	Jul.31	Oct.31	Full Fiscal Year
1986	22.0	22.3	23.0	28.7	96.0
1987	30.5	33.4	33.1	38.1	135.1
1988	44.9	44.5	40.7	48.8	178.9
1989	49.7	50.4	47.6	55.5	203.2
1990	55.0	58.0	56.0	66.0	235

Fiscal Year Ends	EARNINGS PER SHARE A B Jan.31	Apr.30	Jul.31	Oct.31	Full Fiscal Year
1986	.09	.06	.08	.07	.30
1987	.16	.14	.15	.10	.55
1988	.27	.20	.20	.18 F	.86
1989	.32	.23	.24	.20	.99
1990	.33	.26	.29	.27	1.15

Calendar	QUARTERLY DIVIDENDS PAID C Mar.31	Jun.30	Sep.30	Dec.31	Full Year
1986	.042	--	--	--	.04
1987	.053	--	--	--	.05
1988	.112	--	--	--	.11
1989	.16	--	--	--	.16
1990	.20	--	--	--	

BUSINESS: Neutrogena Corporation manufactures and markets premium-priced soaps, specialty skin-care products, and hair care products. Major products include *Neutrogena Soap and Shampoo*; *T/Gel Therapeutic Shampoo and Conditioner*; and *Norwegian Formula Hand Cream*. Int'l op'ns account for 11% of sales. Has subsidiaries in West Germany, France, Japan, and the U.K. Advertising costs: 21% of sales. '89 depreciation rate: 5.2%. Estimated plant age: 10 yrs. Has approximately 1,351 shareholders, 672 employees. Cotsen family controls 44% of the stock; Michell Hutchins Asset Mgmt., 8%; other insiders, 3%. President & Chief Executive Officer: Lloyd Cotsen. Inc.: Delaware. Address: 5755 West 96th Street, Los Angeles, California 90045. Telephone: 213-642-1150.

Neutrogena's first quarter was weaker than we had expected. (Fiscal 1990 ends October 31st.) Net income rose just 4% in the January period, below our estimated increase of 10% and well under the company's earnings growth pace in recent years. A change in the annual promotional cycle, from six two-month intervals to four quarterly periods, resulted in a larger proportion of marketing and selling expenses falling in the first quarter this year. This shift, combined with stiff competition and inventory cutting by retailers, contributed to a 35% decline in *Neutrogena Shampoo and Conditioner* sales. Progress on the international front, meanwhile, was slowed by temporary problems relating to a change in distributors in Great Britain and difficult comparisons in Japan.

We expect earnings momentum to pick up in the second half of fiscal 1990. April-period results will likely again be soft, as retailers continue to adjust to the new promotional program. Earnings also may be hurt by the expense of rolling out a new shampoo and conditioner for permed and color-treated hair. Beginning in the second half, however, the benefits of the new promotional cycles should become more apparent. Furthermore, the rate of increase in marketing and selling costs will subside, since management expects them to remain fairly constant as a percentage of sales for the year. Assuming Neutrogena begins to cultivate modest earnings from the international operations, we estimate earnings will rise 15% in fiscal 1990. These shares are ranked to keep pace with the year-ahead market.

A 20% price drop since our January report has enhanced the long-term case for these shares. Despite the recent quarterly hiccup, Neutrogena continues to introduce excellent products that are well received by consumers and that carry strong credibility with dermatologists. Moreover, most of these offerings still have small market shares, particularly in the skin care area, and the company is steadily widening its distribution network, especially in food stores. Factoring in growing profits overseas, we project 15%-20% annual profit gains to 1992-94. If we're correct, these shares probably will be worthwhile 3- to 5-year performers.
Paul A. Graham, Jr. April 20, 1990

(A) Fiscal year ends Oct. 31st of calendar year. (B) Primary earnings. Excludes extraordinary gain: '89: 1¢. Next earnings report due late May. (C) Next dividend meeting about Dec. 11. 1990: Goes ex about Dec. 18. Approximate dividend payment date: Jan. 12, 1991. (D) Includes intangibles. In '89: $2 mill., $.01/sh. (E) In millions, adjusted for stock splits and dividends. (F) Quarterly numbers don't add to total due to a change in the number of shares outstanding.

Company's Financial Strength	B++
Stock's Price Stability	40
Price Growth Persistence	90
Earnings Predictability	80

Factual material is obtained from sources believed to be reliable, but the publisher is not responsible for any errors or omissions contained herein.

early years, they only paid a penny a share. In 1990, the dividend was increased to 20 cents a share (see 8). Neither Helene Curtis nor Neutrogena are considered income producing stocks. Rather, they are growth stocks. Even though they both pay dividends, the return on market value is minor, especially when you compare it with what your funds could earn in a passbook savings account.

The grand total of all this splitting and stock dividends brings your stock holdings in Neutrogena to 2,784 shares. In dollars and cents at the Value Line quoted price on April 20, 1990 of $23 per share, your overall investment is valued at $64,041 or a 16,010 percent increase from your $400 investment in 1980.

The increase in value in Neutrogena makes the increase in Helene Curtis look like peanuts.

Spotting Winners

How do you spot potential winners? Look at the type of business they do. Are they aggressive in their marketing? Do they bring in new products? Are they appealing to the

---

You should have an expectation—a goal—for every investment. Once you have reached that goal, don't wait around hoping to make an even bigger "killing."

---

baby boom generation? Is it something that is being written up in the newspapers or magazines? Is it a product you can't buy because the stores can't keep it in stock? Or, is it one no one asks for? These are all key questions that need to be addressed.

There's one more thing to look at. If you're interested in aggressive growth, definitely go with a company that has a history of *splitting its shares or paying stock dividends*. Although Helene Curtis paid one stock dividend, Neutrogena did far more. The net result to the share holder is evident.

A Time to Sell

I have already emphasized that timing is all important in buying stocks. It is also all important in selling stocks. One of the mistakes I continually see stock market investors make is to purchase a stock, put it in a drawer and forget about it. Or worse, they actually do notice their stocks dropping week after week but they decide to wait until it "comes up again," to at least gain back the original investment before selling.

Beware of becoming sentimental about your stock. You should have an expectation—a goal—for every investment. Once you have reached that goal, don't wait around hoping to make an even bigger "killing." Conversely, don't stay too long with a stock that has begun to falter while other stocks are prospering. While you may decide to wait out some management growth in a young, aggressive company, remember there's always a right time to sell a stock. Even if you lose some money, you can always deduct the loss on your tax return.

I am not advocating following brokers who roll or turn your account just to get commissions. I am, though, advocating watching your stocks. Watch the overall performance of your portfolio, use your intuition, but remember that intuition is really just a product of experience and observation. There is a limit on every rising stock. Unfortunately, there is no limit on a falling one until you get down to zero.

By now you have a fairly good idea of how and why to use the stock market. But there are still some important terms and concepts that you must be familiar with. It is not necessary to read a book on these concepts just yet, but it will give you that much more leverage to understand a few more terms.

Options. In the stock market, an option is a contract that gives the bearer (you) the right to purchase or sell a specific stock at a specific price within a specific period of time, which is usually nine months. The idea behind options is to give the adventurous speculator the possibility for a maximum involvement in the market, with a potential of high profit at a minimal investment. In other words, leverage. The risks are obvious. But if you win, it can be very exciting.

If you buy an option to purchase a stock at one price and the stock rises above that price, you can either sell the option for a profit, or "exercise" it and buy the stock at the predetermined price. Given the unpredictability of the market, however, the stock could also fall below the option price. If this happens, your investment is lost.

The permutations of the option market are almost endless and beyond the scope of this book. If you have an interest in trading options, you can directly contact the Chicago Board of Options or any major brokerage firm, and receive one or several of the detailed pamphlets that explain various strategies available. Much here will depend upon your attitude toward investment risk and willingness to pay close attention to the day-to-day changes in stock prices. One final word: Not all stocks trade in the option exchanges. Usually larger companies that have ongoing activity in their stocks are available for option trading.

Commodities. Everywhere you look, there are commodities: potatoes, wheat, chickens, plywood, corn, cocoa, sugar, gold, even financial futures. Because supply and demand are in a constant fluctuation, there is money to be made *and lost* in speculating on what the availability and demand will be over a course of time.

Suppliers of commodities like to know what they will receive for their produce on a given date. They, therefore, are sellers of the commodity. The buyer may be you. When you buy a commodity contract, you agree to pay a certain amount for a specific amount of the commodity on a specific date. When you come to terms, a contract is created and traded on the open market. Now, that seems fairly straightforward, but there are a variety of factors—the unpredictable weather, consumer tastes, politics and even financial conditions can affect the commodity market. It becomes a very volatile investment. You can even lose more than what you start with!

In commodities, a small percentage is required as a down payment—a form of a good faith payment. If the commodity goes up, it's wonderful. You are truly leveraged and can make a significant amount of money. On the other hand, it can fall the other way. If a commodity drops significantly in price (guaranteed, they all will go up and down), then not only could your contract lose value, but you could actually lose not only your deposit, or good faith money, but more. Remember, leverage works both ways.

The commodity market is a classic example of the

maxim: The higher the degree of risk, the greater the degree of return. I like to also keep in mind the other maxim: What goes up, must come down. In my opinion, only two types of women should participate in the commodities market—the farmer, to hedge her crops for future delivery and sale; and the woman who has lots, and I mean lots, of money to burn. If that fits your description, then enjoy! Otherwise, this is another area you avoid like the plague.

Preferred Stock. Many companies also offer preferred stock. The primary difference is that preferred stock is entitled to a fixed dividend before the common stock gets paid. It does not change if a company does well via an increased pay-out. If a company is not doing well, it could be eliminated or deferred for a specific period of time. Who decides? The company's board of directors.

There are three types of preferred stock; *straight preferred,* which pays a fixed dividend and has seniority over the common stock. The second type is *convertible preferred,* a hybrid. It allows the preferred shareholder to convert her shares into common stock at an already predetermined price. Why would you want to do that? If the company is doing well, it will allow you to exchange your stock for the common shares and more than likely benefit in two ways. One, the possibility of a greater dividend return, since it can be increased, and two, the market value per share can increase if the underlying company does well at a greater rate than regular preferred stock.

An example of this second type is AT&T. In the 1970s, AT&T's common stock paid less than its preferred shares. As time passed and before the divestiture of the company, its earnings had increased significantly. Eventually, the dividend for the common stock exceeded the preferred dividend payment. Over a 10-year period, the common stock dividend per share had increased almost $2 over its regular dividend payment. Correspondingly the market value per share increased approximately 25 percent.

The third type of preferred stock is *cumulative preferred*. With this, you have a safety valve for the investor. If, for whatever reason, a company has a bad time and has to eliminate or defer its dividend, there is hope for recovery. When the company begins paying preferred dividends at a later date, it must make up for all the dividends it missed. Keep in mind a company cannot pay a common share dividend and bypass the preferred. The preferred has seniority.

Investing in preferred stocks rarely offers growth potential, with the exception of the convertible preferred issue. If you want income, this may be your cup of tea. Otherwise, I would invest in the common stock.

Brokers and Discount Brokers. A broker is the agent who handles *buy and sell orders* for you in both securities and commodities transactions. In exchange, he or she will receive a commission for advice and related services. Some brokers, known as full-service brokers, provide research, recommendations, even warnings. Their counterpart is a discount broker who makes no recommendations although fully licensed to do so. They merely carry out your orders to buy or sell and do so at a lower fee than the fuller service broker. The disadvantage is that they give no advice, nor do they sell shares in tax shelters of other forms of limited partnerships. But then, that could be an advantage.

A few years ago, investors nationwide voted that the

number one brokerage house was Charles Schwab & Company, a discount broker. Why? Their service was the best.

SUMMING IT UP

By now, you should realize there can be value, excitement and choice in the stock market. You can go far toward matching your personality and interest with solid investment goals. But you can also go too far. The market has always risen and dropped—gone higher and dipped again.

The market does offer exciting opportunities, but you are also advised to heed the advice found in Ecclesiastes 5:13-16: "There is another serious problem I have seen everywhere—savings are put into risky investments that turn sour, and soon there is nothing left to pass on to one's son. The man who speculates is soon back to where he began—with nothing . . . . He has been working for the wind. It is all swept away."

Before you invest your funds, understand the risks involved. What has the stock done in the past? Is the present "market climate" conducive to overall investing? What do the stock market analysts project? And finally, do you know anything about the product the company makes?

If you can get information to satisfy each question, the investment may be the right one for you. On the other hand, if there are gaps or holes, be wise and pass.

CHAPTER TEN
Mutual Benefits from Mutual Funds

Mutual funds might well have been included in the conclud-
ing pages of the last chapter. But mutual funds can offer
some significant benefits over individual stocks, and so
rate a chapter of their own.

The definition of a mutual fund is easy: It is a pooled
investment in a large number of companies—their stocks
or bonds. It is an investment cooperative wherein your
stock represents a share in a large portfolio of diverse individual stocks. The decision to buy a mutual fund can be
equally easy, for many investors buy into a fund solely
because it does represent many companies. It's one way
to achieve diversification.

Diversification and Protection Go Hand in Hand

An old adage in the money game is, "When in doubt, diversify, diversify, diversify." The importance of this cannot be

overstated, for diversification, or hedging, offers significant protection in uncertain and changing financial times. The warning of Ecclesiastes 11:2, written back in the tenth century B.C., still holds, "Divide your gifts among many, for in the days ahead you yourself may need much help." The older *Revised Standard Version* wording is even more explicit, "Give a portion to seven, or even to eight for you know not what evil may happen on earth."

For busy women who haven't the time nor the skill to study and pick their own stocks, mutual funds offer professional management.

Large-scale stock market investors don't entrust all their capital to a few securities. They diversify, carefully selecting a broad range of stocks. Many even include mutual funds within their portfolios. Medium-sized investors like the planned diversification of mutual funds. And for the smaller investor who hasn't the capital to buy stock in several companies, the mutual fund allows her to invest a small amount of money in a large number of different securities. Many funds allow initial investments as low as $100.

Do as the Experts Do

Another related advantage to mutual funds is expertise. For busy women who haven't the time nor the skill to study and pick their own stocks, mutual funds offer professional management. It is not only acceptable, it is often wise to rely on other people. Ecclesiastes says, "Two can accomplish more than twice as much as one, for the results can be much better" (4:9).

Funds need to be watched like any other stock. But by and large most successfully follow consistent investment strategies based on extensive research. They decide when and where to trade securities, give you the option of regular cash payments or automatic reinvestment of earnings, and even do the paperwork needed for the IRS.

Open vs. Closed

Another advantage is liquidity. There are two types of mutual funds. An *open-ended fund* has an infinite number of shares. The more money that's put into the fund, the more shares are created. Open-ended shares are traded at a price determined by the net asset value of the fund. Thus the price is a direct reflection of the performance of that fund and the performance of the different stocks within that fund. You can cash in holdings in open-ended funds for their underlying asset value at a moment's notice. Your check for the proceeds will be in the mail within seven days.

Closed-ended funds have a limited number of shares that are traded on the market, the price being determined by supply and demand. They must be sold on an exchange, like ordinary stock. Their shares are as liquid as the open-ended funds.

Reading the values or quotes in your newspaper is not difficult. In a reprint of closing quotations for Fidelity's Magellan Fund from the *Wall Street Journal,* dated May 22, 1987, note the difference in price[2], the increase in value from the day before[1], and the abbreviation of name.[3]

	Sell	Buy	Chg
Fidelity Investments[3]		[2]	[1]
Mageln	51.10	52.68	+.39

In other words, if you want to buy Fidelity's Magellan Fund, you would pay $52.68 per share. If you choose to sell or liquidate your shares, you would receive $51.10 per share, a difference of $1.58. The Magellan Fund increased in value 39 cents from the preceding day, or from $50.71 to $51.10 and $52.29 to $52.68, respectively.

In probing further, you learn that the Magellan Fund

More and more investors are looking for opportunities that are not only financially sound, but also meet their own needs, temperaments and ideals.

---

has a minimum investment requirement of $1,000. For an IRA, the minimum required is $250, not $1000.

Reducing the Load

In addition, mutual funds can be distinguished as "load" or "no-load" funds. A load fund is one in which a commission is charged on the purchase, the amount of the commission varying with the money invested: about 8-½ percent for the first $10,000, perhaps 7-½ percent for the next $10,000. Be wary of brokers who urge you to take one large sum and divide it among two, three or more different load funds. That's a highly unethical way of making a large commission. A broker makes more money from three 8-½ percent commissions on $10,000 than from a reduced commission rate for a single $30,000 transaction. In the Fidelity Magellan Fund example above, a 3 percent load is charged.

Obviously, if you buy into a load fund, you should plan to keep your money invested for a fairly long term. The commission charged on each transaction discourages investors from hopping from one fund to the next. That's why I urge my clients who wish to invest in mutual funds to do so in funds that actually contain a family of varying portfolios, each with a different objective. If you should decide you'd like to move your money from a growth-oriented fund to an income-producing fund, you could do so without paying additional commission. You might think a no-load fund would be most advantageous. Remember, though, there is no free lunch. If there's not a load charge, there will be a management fee of some sort.

An Age of Specialists

There is one more advantage in using a mutual fund, one that could have particular relevance for the Christian. This is the trend toward specialized funds. More and more investors are looking for opportunities that are not only financially sound, but also meet their own needs, temperaments and ideals. It is one investment area where you can exercise some ethical or moral control. "And we know that all that happens to us is working for our good if we love God and are fitting into his plans" (Rom. 8:28).

I do not believe it's wrong for a Christian to make an investment solely for financial consideration; a stronger financial base will always work to leave you freer for chosen work. But, if it's important to consider social needs, here is a place. If you feel strongly, for instance, about investing even marginally in the military, you can choose a defense-oriented fund. If you resent the perceived elitism or arbitrary bureaucracy of companies like IBM, you can select a fund that invests only in small companies.

A sector fund invests in a single industry, such as health-care, transportation or financial services. There are gold-oriented funds or science-and-technology funds. Global funds invest in both foreign and U.S. companies; international funds invest entirely in foreign securities; single-country funds focus on the securities of one country. Mutual funds, in other words, come in all shapes, sizes and colors.

Too Much for So Many

Many experts feel mutual funds are a proliferation of funds and have created confusion. Indeed, with some 370 new funds launched in 1986 alone, more funds existed in early 1987 than there were companies on the New York Stock Exchange. Not only are there many funds, there is a lot of market hype and gimmickery involved in the increasingly competitive promotion of each one. However, the determined investor can, with a little research, find the funds that are right for her. "Be sure that everything is done properly in a good and orderly way" (1 Cor. 14:40). "Work hard and cheerfully at all you do, just as though you were working for the Lord and not merely for your masters" (Col. 3:23).

The Guiding Light

There are several significant guideposts that will help in choosing a mutual fund. Ultimately, results are the final test—the measurement that might forgive all the confusion and hype and high fees. Fund performance must at least keep up with inflation. Consider the average return figure over the last five years, keeping in mind that in investment circles it is traditionally believed the top-performing fund of the year rarely repeats its performance the next year.

Weisenberger Investment Companies Service

The Weisenberger Investment Companies Service is an excellent resource, providing past and current performances of all mutual funds. It is available at brokerage firms and most libraries. The Securities and Exchange Commission (SEC) has recently inaugurated rules to standardize yield calculations for bond funds and to require all funds to advertise their total returns, minus commissions and fees, over 5-year periods. One obvious drawback to buying into a new fund is that it lacks a track record to compare with either the overall market or with other funds of its type.

Simple Resources Reduce Confusion

Two other sources are available on your newsstand or by subscription. *Money* magazine is a monthly publication that's a must for any woman interested in having her money grow. In the fall, it brings out its annual review of all the funds, ranks them, comments on strengths and weaknesses of management and compares previous years' performances. The best part? It's in understandable English! *Forbes* magazine, a biweekly publication, issues a special fund edition every August. *Forbes* is a real asset for the mutual fund investor. It does much the same as *Money* magazine, but it includes another ingredient—it ranks the fund's performance in a good stock market *and* in a bad stock market. If it's an *A* it's terrific, but an *F* means avoid it like the plague.

I prefer to go with a fund that is rated *A* or better in a bad market and *B* or better in a good market. Why? Almost anyone can make money when the market is great, but the real pros shine when things aren't so hot. With this method, you eliminate almost 85 percent of the funds. With all the chances you have, you need a starting point—this is a good one.

Follow the Road Map

Another guidepost is found in the prospectus of a mutual fund. This will state what the fund's objectives are, as well as give a breakdown of what it has invested in. Use it as a road map. It's not exciting reading—it's more like a cure for insomnia—but it does tell you who they are, how they have done, how much money is under management and what kind of skeletons are lurking out there. Even though a prospectus is only published every 13 months, and will not give you a totally accurate fix on where the monies are at any given time, it will give valuable insight for your investment strategy.

Primary Fund Categories

Growth. The biggest group, these funds typically buy shares of more established companies as they seek to achieve long-term capital appreciation.

Growth and Income. Such funds invest in stocks with a

dividend kicker on top of appreciation potential.

Income. Their main appeal is high dividends, which often come from holding utility stocks or preferred shares.

Bond. Corporate, U.S. government and tax-free municipal bond funds are among the subcategories. Junk-bond funds, which invest in low-rated but high yielding debt securities, are a current favorite because they still command double-digit interest returns. However, there is a big *but* here: junk means risk, sometimes excessive. Look carefully before you leap.

Specialty Funds. The newest kids on the block fall into this category. Anything you can imagine—health, energy, computer, communication, precious metals, international, money, even commodities, are just a few of your choices. A health-oriented fund will only buy stocks in the health care and related industries. Some will be growth, others income and others combined in their objectives. There is truly something out there for everyone in this category.

Other Sources

A number of directories list funds by investment goal and give details on purchase requirements. A guide to funds with small or no sales commissions is available for $5 from the No-Load Mutual Fund Association, P.O. Box 2004, JAF Building, New York, NY 10116. A compilation of commission and commission-free funds is available for $1 from the Investment Company Institute, 1600 M Street, N.W., Washington, D.C. 20036, Attention: Guide. Or visit your local library. The reference section will be your guide.

Make sure you use information that has been updated or revised within the last year.

The Ten Commandments of Mutual Fund Investing

Success requires a plan—*your* money plan. Now that you have the basics, use these 10 rules as a guide in your quest to conquer and evaluate the many options you have to choose from:

1. The best return is what you are after. Use a *no-load fund*. Historically, load funds have not outperformed no-load funds. If you selected a load fund instead, a heavy penalty is paid if you withdraw soon after purchase.
2. Don't pick a small fund group. Select a family in the $100 to $300 million range. They can afford to hire the best managers.
3. Avoid disaster. Review the fund's performance in the 1973-1974 and 1981-1982 periods. The majority of funds did miserably. See if yours did at least better than the pack.
4. Avoid last year's winner. Murphy's Law says it won't be number one this year.
5. Avoid a fund that has a peak and valley record. As long as it stays ahead of the averages, you will win. Sudden lurches lead to queasy stomachs, which lead to emotional bailouts, often at the wrong times.
6. Determine if there has been a change of management or philosophy that might damage future performances. Often companies are bought because

they do so well. The new team may not have the Midas touch.

7. Be wary of brand new funds. Why risk an unknown? If you are anxious to try something new, consider a fund whose manager has achieved a respected reputation elsewhere. Be wary of clone funds, as in the Lookalike Fund and the Lookalike Fund 2. Rarely is the portfolio manager the same.

8. Reinvest all gains and dividends.

9. Commit to regular investing over a period of time.

10. If in doubt, spread your risk in several funds.

Would You Rather Switch?

You may not want to invest in funds designed to seek the largest gains; maybe you'll feel more comfortable with a conservative fund, perhaps a large, traditional growth fund or family of funds. My choice for you would be the family—a fund group, which has several funds under its umbrella—a money fund, some of the specialty funds, an income fund, and oh, yes, don't forget the growth. The family concept allows you to switch from one fund to another with nominal charges—$5 to $10. After all, what does well this year may not do well next year. Whatever your position, there is plenty of information readily available to help you.

The traditional approach is to buy and hold: Select funds and stick with them through interim market gyrations and purchase additional shares at regular intervals. Some analysts, however, advise switching among funds to always be with the latest winners. Market-timing strategists go even further. They use formulas to gauge the market's strength and advise jumping between stock funds and money market funds. Their idea is to be out of stock funds when stocks are weak and, instead, earn interest in money funds.

You can be your own analyst. You don't need an expensive service for advice. Review the tips on spotting trends in chapter 2, sharpen your pencil and do your own switching.

Mutual funds are not the ultimate answer, nor the solution to your investment needs, but they should be an ingredient in your financial plan. Your age, tax status, investment philosophy, as well as personal philosophy, will all influence your final decision.

CHAPTER ELEVEN
Bonds—Investing Through Lending

The bond market is similar to the stock market with one major exception: With a bond, you are *loaning* monies *to* an entity rather than investing monies *in* an entity. That entity is often a corporation, large enough to be a household word or smaller, perhaps specializing in an area with which you are unfamiliar. Whereas a stock represents ownerships, a bond is merely a loan, an IOU from a corporation or government municipality. Loans by definition are perilous.

Proverbs 20:16 warns, "It is risky to make loans to strangers!" And as we have noted in chapter 3, it can be even riskier to make loans to family or friends. But nonetheless, there is some financial value in the concept of a loan, and the bond market allows you, as an investor, a method of making a loan while substantially reducing the risk of a loan.

REDUCING THE RISK

There are two ways a bond reduces the risk of a loan. The first is by *allowing you some sound information about the organization's credit worthiness.* Sometimes bonds are secured or backed by collateral. A particular model of aircraft could serve as collateral for a bond issued by an airplane company. If the company fails to pay timely interest, the bondholder's agent has the right to sell assets to recoup investment. But more often, bonds are issued on the good faith and general reliability of the corporation or

---

A rule of thumb to keep in mind is that the higher the rate of return, the greater the degree of risk.

---

municipality. These bonds are known as GOs—general obligations. Before a company can pay dividends to its stockholders it must pay all the interest and principal due on bonds. But if it fails to pay, the bondholder's only recourse is to force the company into bankruptcy. "Be sure you know a person well," says Proverbs 11:15, "before you vouch for his credit! Better refuse than suffer later."

There are many ways to get to "know" who is issuing a certain bond. First, all bonds are sold by prospectus through a securities broker. You should examine this right away before you send in your dollars. Second, both Standard and Poor's and Moody's Investment Service rate all entities that issue bonds, from the best *AAA* on down. You can also get a good idea of the credit worthiness of a corporation by comparing the interest rates offered on its bonds to those issued by others. The less reliable the company (or city), the higher the interest it will have to pay in order to attract buyers for the bonds.

A company with the very best credit, like Exxon or IBM, is often able to sell bonds that pay only a percentage point more than, say, treasury bonds. Other companies that are not in the blue chip league may be forced to pay 3 or 4 percentage points more than Uncle Sam. The trade-offs of a few percentage points in income versus a stronger sense of security are up to you, but at least the bond market gives you enough information to make an informed choice. A rule of thumb to keep in mind is that the higher the rate of return, the greater the degree of risk.

The second way bonds reduce the risk of a loan is by *guaranteeing a specific rate of interest for a specific time.* A bond is an interest-only loan. You are promised interest twice a year with full payback anywhere from 3 months (treasury bills) to 30 years plus (more the norm). Although the value of the bond itself may fluctuate, you never have to guess about your income during the time you hold it. And if you hold it the full term, your principal payback is also guaranteed. That is, unless the company fails. If you stick with known companies that are rated *AA* or *AAA,* there should be no problems.

BUYING IN

Bonds, then, offer certain safety margins. They also offer certain trading opportunities, for bonds are very much a marketable commodity. They are bought and sold on the stock exchange and their value rises or falls depending on factors such as the maturity date of the bond and the interest rate being paid.

If current interest rates are around 10 percent, then that's the rate an issuing corporation would pay for new money. If the interest rate rose, new bonds might pay 10-½ percent. A 9-½ percent bond would be less attractive, since a newer bond of comparable quality would be paying a significantly higher rate. Suppose, however, that the interest rates dipped to 7-½ percent. Top rate bonds might pay about 8 percent and the 9-½ percent bond would sell at a premium, not at a discount.

Another rule of thumb is that as interest rates rise, bonds become less valuable on the market. The reverse is true as interest rates decline.

If a bond is selling at its original offering price, it is known as trading *at par*. If a bond is selling below its original price, it is *discounted*. To compete with a new issue 10-½ percent bond, a 9-½ percent bond would have to be discounted or sold at less than par value.

Highly discounted bonds are often called "junk bonds." These have an additional stigma besides interest rate fluctuation; the term generally refers to companies that cannot meet the rating services' criteria for safety and stability, companies that are in trouble, perhaps on the verge of bankruptcy. But don't be fooled. More often than not the title may be undeserved. There are significant gains to be made with junk bonds. Except in the direst situation, the extra value and interest to be earned may be enough to compensate investors for taking a chance. Note, however, that junk bonds are difficult to research and are less liquid. One alternative way to buy them is through a mutual fund that specializes in junk bonds.

New bonds at their original issue will cost $1,000 per bond. After their offering the current market and economic environment will be major factors in their pricing until final maturity. So, what starts at $1,000 per bond, can dip to $825, $950, $600 or lower; or, it can trade at over $1,000. At maturity, the price will settle at $1,000.

If you believe interest rates will fluctuate over the years or that there will be changes in the economic and/or political environment, don't buy bonds, stick them in a drawer and forget about them. You will miss several opportunities to take a profit by selling as interest rates drop and buying again when rates increase. One thing I can guarantee: The rate will change many, many times in your ownership period.

Many bond funds offer minimum buy-ins for a few hundred dollars. Check management performance, per my recommendations in chapter 10 on mutual funds.

The listing of bonds on a bond exchange usually looks like this:

BOND	CURRENT YIELD	SALES IN $1,000S	HIGH	LOW	LAST	NET CHG
GMILLS 8s99	12	3	69	70½	69	—1

This General Mills bond, due to mature in 1999, is paying eight percent, or $80, in interest per year on each $1,000 bond. The current yield is the interest payment divided by the current price of the bond. If the current yield is higher than the stated coupon interest rate, you know that the bond is selling at a discount. The volume (in sales of $1,000s) was three: just three $1,000 bonds were sold, at prices ranging from $690 (69 percent of $1,000) to $705 (70.5 percent of $1,000). Net change means that the bond is down $10 (.10 × 1,000) from the day before.

This example shows a remarkably low-volume issue, a "thin" issue. This isn't unusual, but it does indicate just how illiquid a bond can be. In general, it is wiser to stick with issues that have relatively large markets. You do not want to find yourself in a situation where when you want to sell, few want to buy. Your selling could actually push the price down due to a greater volume than what is considered "normal" on a given day.

It is often hard for investors to look at new bonds with maturation dates 20 or 30 years distant. It is indicative of the outlook of modern investors that the terms of recent bond issues have become shorter and shorter. People seem more unwilling to have their money committed for a long period of time, especially in an era of rising inflation and interest rates, when the market for bonds is weak.

CALLING AHEAD

It is wise to check the *call* provision in the bond contract. This gives the company the option to redeem the bond at a specific price after a specific date. Call provisions work entirely to the issuer's advantage. If the market price of the bond remains below the call price, which is typically $30 or $40 greater than the $1,000 face value, the bond is never redeemed. However, if interest rates fall sharply, the company can call it back at original face value and borrow the money at a lower cost. This may not be good news to you. Lower interest rates mean your bond will sell at a premium. If the company calls it back, you will lose the premium and the higher yield you are enjoying on your money.

It's important, then, to know exactly what the call provision says before buying a bond. Better still, buy bonds (as in the General Mills bond sample above) that are selling well below face value. That way, if interest rates fall, you, rather than the issuer, will enjoy the windfall as the bond rises in price.

A final thought. In the last few years, corporations have begun to issue bonds with *put* provisions, the buyer's version of a call. They typically give the owner the right to sell bonds back to the issuer at face value after four or five years have elapsed. This put provision doesn't come free; figure you'll get about a percentage point less interest. But the put may well be worth the price since it locks in a floor value for the bond, no matter how much interest rates change. This floor value is usually placed at a comfortable premium over the original issue price.

CONVERTIBLE AND ZERO COUPON BONDS

There are two additional designations of corporate bonds. One is the *convertible bond.* This means that the bond can be converted to shares of common stock at a predetermined price. Thus, the price of the convertible bond is tied into the price of the stock. Obviously the option of converting to common stock is worthless if the stock is selling on the market at a price well below that specified on the bond.

Zero coupon bonds are securities that accumulate interest until maturity rather than paying it to the owner on a regular basis. Zeros are sold at discount from their face value with the discount reflecting the interest that will be earned on the way to maturity. The big draw here is the chance to invest a little, then, thanks to the miracle of compound interest, to come back decades later and collect what could be a small fortune. If you buy a 12 percent zero coupon bond today, due to mature in 20 years, you pay $97.22. In 20 years you get back $1,000. The longer the time to maturity and the higher the interest rate, the greater the "miracle" of return. It is noteworthy, however, that inflation could—indeed is likely to—reduce the purchasing power of the face value to less spectacular sums.

Still, zeros are more than a marketing gimmick because they offer a certainty of return. Compare a zero to an ordinary bond paying the same 12 percent for the same 20 years. With the ordinary bond, you know you'll get $120 in interest every year. But you won't know what return you'll be able to earn on the $120 should you wish to reinvest it. In contrast, with a 20-year zero coupon bond, you are assured a 12 percent return on accumulated interest, as well as 12 percent on the principal.

This feature makes zero coupon bonds particularly attractive to managers of pension funds and insurance companies, who know they must deliver X dollars a month to a specific number of people 26 years down the road. And it is catching on with individual investors who are accumulating capital for some distant goal like retirement or kids' education, and want to know exactly how much they'll end up with.

Catch 22

Note one other disadvantage—no, call it what it is, a trick. Some tax exempt zeros are being issued with call provisions that give the issuer the option of buying back the bonds below par. That's just unfair, since the whole point of a zero is to be able to lock-in yield.

Do not buy zeros if you need your funds in a short period of time—less than five years. They are interest sensitive and feel the effect of a rising interest market greater than a straight corporate bond. Your value will drop—a lot and very quickly. This is due to the smaller initial amounts of money involved. In other words, leverage. On the other

---

A-*rated and better bonds can be very safe investments. They pay a lower interest rate than corporate bonds, but because of their tax favored status they are most valuable to those in higher tax brackets.*

---

hand, if interest rates drop, you will enjoy a sharp increase in value.

MUNICIPAL AND FEDERAL BONDS

We have mentioned that bonds can be issued by municipalities as well as by corporations. Municipal bonds can be issued by a state, a city or a municipal entity such as a water commission, a transportation authority, or an educational facility. The interest from these bonds is exempt from federal taxes. If the bonds are issued by an entity in the state where you are a resident, the interest is also exempt from state taxes.

At times you may have trouble finding out what you need to know about the occasionally obscure governmental authorities that issue municipal bonds; and their balance sheets can be difficult to interpret. But *A*-rated and better bonds can be very safe investments. They pay a lower interest rate than corporate bonds, but because of their tax favored status they are most valuable to those in higher tax brackets. To get the full benefits of a tax-free bond, you should be paying taxes; otherwise, buy corporate bonds. The interest will be at a higher rate.

UNCLE SAM IS IN THE MARKET

The U.S. Treasury is the primary issuer of bonds backed by the U.S. government. These are fixed-yield securities with maturities ranging from 91 days to 30 years. Those that mature in 10 years or more are called treasury bonds (in contrast to the shorter-term treasury bills and notes). Institutions and big companies are the largest buyers of federal securities, but about 20 percent are purchased by individuals. Treasury bonds can be attractive and conservative investments. Government backing makes them free of risk of default, but not of risks associated with interest rate changes. They are highly liquid, are generally sold for modest fees, if any, and are free of state and local, but not federal, taxes.

There is a tremendously active secondary market for treasury bonds, so you can sell them quickly if necessary. They represent quick cash with interest up to date of sale. Their exemption from state and local taxes insures a fast, uniform market throughout the country. You don't have to worry about a thin or lightly traded market here.

Treasury bonds are listed slightly differently than corporate bonds. The quote below was in the *Wall Street Journal* on June 15, 1987.

RATE	DATE	BID	ASKED	CHG.	YIELD
11¾	2005—10 Feb	127	127.8	+2.9	8.70

The coupon rate on this bond is 11-¾ percent, meaning the Treasury will pay the owner $117.50 a year, in two payments six months apart. The bond matures in either February 2005 or 2010. When two dates are listed, as in this example, the government reserves the option to pay back the face values to the owners at the earlier date.

The *bid* is the price dealers are willing to pay for the bond, with the digits in front of the decimal referring to the percentage of face value. Just to keep you on your toes, the numbers after the decimal point aren't decimals at all, but thirty-seconds of a percentage point. So a bid of 127 translates as 127 percent of $1,000, or $1,270.00.

The *asked* column shows the price at which dealers are willing to sell. In this case, it's 1,272.50, or $2.50 more than they would pay for the bond (127.8 = 1270 and 8/32, or 2.50). *Chg.* refers to the change in the bid price from the previous day, again in thirty-seconds of a percentage point of face value. The *Wall Street Journal* reported "+2.9." This means the bid price of the bond rose 2-9/32 of $10, or $22.81. (2 = $20; $10 ÷ 32 = .3125; .3125 × 9 = 2.8125. Now, add the $20 to $2.81 and you arrive at $22.81.) Got it? You are now at the head of the class. Most don't have a clue as to how pricing works.

The *Yield* column is the annual interest yield—in this case expressed with honest-to-goodness decimals—that an owner would receive by purchasing the bond for the *asked* price and holding it to maturity in 2010. Note that 8.70 percent is quite a bit less than the 11-3/4 percent coupon rate. That's because the bond is selling above the face value, or at a premium.

If you want to sell treasuries, you go to some of the largest national brokerage houses, who likely have offices near you. These firms have gone into actively trading treasuries for their own account and deal with the Federal

Reserve. They will very likely make you a *net* bid—no commission, because they'll buy from you for their trading account. Your bank can also handle transactions, as the brokerage house does, at a fee of $25 to $50.

A DIFFERENT AUCTION

Treasuries are usually sold at weekly auctions held through the Federal Reserve Banks, and announced in advance. You can go to or phone the nearest Federal Reserve Bank or branch and get full information on how to participate in the auction, although you do not personally attend. It is important to tell officials at the bank that you are a private investor and want to bid non-competitively.

They will want a good faith deposit before the sale to insure you are serious and will follow through. On the day of the sale, the big institutional buyers submit their bids, and the securities are sold at the least interest cost to the Treasury. There will be a range of prices they will accept to sell the whole issue to the competitive bidders and still have some for the private sector. Your price will be the average of the competitive bids they accept.

The bids received are fed into a central computer to see who gets how many at what price, and to figure the average price—the one that is important to you. The results are announced in the next day's news. At this time, if you have made a purchase, be sure you pay the balance and carry out your contract on the day the bonds are ready for delivery. The details of your transaction will be confirmed immediately after the auction.

Both the announcements of sales and results are broadcast to the press, but only newspapers with good financial sections or the *Wall Street Journal* publish them.

If you don't live near a Federal Reserve Bank or branch, you can write the one nearest you for information on what procedure to follow to buy treasuries. You should do this well in advance of when you want to enter an order so you'll be prepared when an issue comes along that you think you'd like to buy into. Your library, bank or Chamber of Commerce can provide you with the address of the nearest Federal Reserve Bank.

OTHER FEDERAL BONDS

While Treasury securities are direct obligations of the federal government, there are a number of federal agencies that issue bonds. These include the Federal Land Bank, Federal Home Loan Bank, Federal National Mortgage Association (Fannie Mae) and Government National Mortgage Association (Ginnie Mae). There are many other agencies within the federal government that issue bonds. Quotations and issues can be found in the *Wall Street Journal* under Government Agency Issues.

There are many maturities and a fairly active trading market on all of these. As usual the yields are greater in the issues that have a longer maturity date.

If you're interested, there are so many of these bonds that you should look them up in technical books available in most libraries. One kind of bond is the *Ginnie Mae,* a strange hybrid security with a combination of interest and pay-back of principal.

In 1970 when home mortgages were hard to obtain and then only at extremely high interest rates, Congress formed the Government National Mortgage Association to aid both the building industry and the many people needing to build homes. It is a pool of many single-family mortgages, and the pool is backed by the GNMA and Federal Housing Administration—Veteran's Administration. Investors can buy certificates in the pool without worry about their investment, and get their money in the form of interest and principal repayments without the trouble of collections, possible foreclosures or the like. That work is all done for them, hence the certificates are known as "pass-throughs."

The pool receives payments on homeowner's mortgages, which include both interest and a payment on the principal. As you receive your payments from the pool, part of it is taxable interest.

Experience has shown that on the average, home mortgages get paid off within 12 years. If every mortgage in the pool just paid the monthly interest and principal, each check you get would be partially interest, the remainder principal. But each time a mortgage is refinanced, or prepaid by the homeowner, principal is distributed in advance as an "extra" to the certificate holders. This, and the regular installments on principal, are not taxable. Just your proportional share of the pool's interest receipts.

Originally, the lowest amount you could buy from a broker was $100,000. But now several large brokerage firms may buy a million or more dollars' worth and offer certificates of participation as small as $10,000. These can be very interesting to retirees, or those planning to retire soon, for three reasons. First, they are safe. Second, they offer high return. Third, your involvement, once you've made the purchase, is minimal. Of course, when you've received back all the money you invested as principal, that's the end. But as your principal receipts or "extras" get substantial, you can reinvest them, possibly in stocks.

THE CHOICE IS YOURS

Fixed principal plus fluctuating income, or fixed income plus fluctuating principal. Which is the better choice? The answer depends on the needs of the investor and the difference in interest rates paid on long- and short-term securities. If you are saving for a down payment on a house, preservation of principal is more important than certain knowledge of the amount of interest you'll earn next year. On the other hand, investors who can bear to take the risk might want to invest a substantial portion of their savings in long-term securities that pay two or three percentage points more interest than the shorter term alternative.

Deuteronomy 15:1,2 cautions:

> At the end of every seventh year there is to be a canceling of all debts! Every creditor shall write "Paid in full" on any promissory note he holds.

Few bonds have maturities of less than 10 years—but they do exist. Ask your financial planner, stock broker or mutual fund information office about short-term obligations. Don't stretch or loan your monies out for long periods of time. The advice from Scripture is well-taken.

In today's economy, for most people, the right choice is compromise, mixing short- and long-term securities. The choice is yours.

CHAPTER TWELVE

Real Estate: Realistic Risks with Real Returns

One of the highest investment returns you can get is in real estate. I know this is a sweeping statement, but there's really no argument against it. The amount of money made on real estate investments has increased steadily, sometimes with great leaps and bounds, at other times, just a few percent a year. Although the wealthy families of this country may have made their money originally in steel, oil, railroads or banking, virtually every one has enhanced their fortunes by investing in real estate. Managed with care, real estate can be your best investment.

The advantages of real estate begin with the fact that land and buildings are solid, visible, easily understood. The intrinsic value of real estate is as old as humanity itself. As early as 1400 B.C., Moses recognized that wealth and value resided in land. When the Lord instructed Moses to divide up the land of Israel by lot, the men of the tribe of Joseph complained that when daughters were given land, it would pass into the hands of the tribe into which they married. Moses decreed, "Let [the daughters of Zelophehad] be married to anyone they like, so long as it is within their own tribe" (Num. 36:6,7).

Available land does not change, but population and need for space do. The law of supply and demand con-

---

A homeowner can contribute to the appreciation of her net worth merely by taking normal care of her own home.

---

tinues and will continue to increase the value of land and that which is placed on the land. The Bible counsels youth:

> To . . . take care of their own homes (1 Tim. 5:14).

> An empty stable stays clean—but there is no income from an empty stable (Prov. 14:4).

> A man who strays from home is like a bird that wanders from its nest (27:8).

> Wisdom has built a palace supported on seven pillars (9:1).

The financial advantages of real estate are equally solid. There can be a high rate of return, substantially above inflation. Tax benefits are still available, assuming you invest in land with a building on it, not raw land. And real estate has leverage, or the ability to own, for all practical purposes, a piece of property you have not completely paid for. Based on these advantages, let's look specifically at some of the real estate investments you might make.

YOUR OWN HOME

Your first real estate will probably be your own home. While it might be a mistake to tie yourself to a house too soon, home ownership should be a primary investment goal. Renting may seem simple, but renters are not in control of their own long-term housing costs. They have no stake in the inflationary spiral, and they derive no income tax benefits from their housing payments. Further, the pride and care normally given to one's home is providing no net worth value to the renter. A homeowner can contribute to the appreciation of her net worth merely by taking normal care of her own home.

The *return* on your own home comes primarily from its appreciation over the years. Unquestionably, much of a home's value is implicit, weighed in personal terms based on location, neighborhood, shape, size, maintenance, privacy, aesthetics, etc. But there is explicit value as well.

One measure of bedrock value is the cost of replacing your house with a comparable structure. If you own a conventional house in a pleasant neighborhood, you can safely assume that neither property values nor construction costs are going to fall. This year's $100,000 house could easily be next year's $112,000 house.

Consider that an average house costing $26,000 in 1968 was $58,000 in 1978. Even after the dollar's diminishing buying power (inflation) is taken into account, the seller of that average house still showed a profit of $4,500 in 1968 dollars, or nearly $10,000 in 1978 terms.

The bottom line is that inflation will probably be with us for many years to come, and since the residence is the best investment vehicle for a family, the higher the asset value a family can control, the better. A $60,000 house is fine, but if you can afford it, a $120,000 house could appreciate at a much greater rate.

Certainly, I am not advising over-extension. The Bible tells us to be content with what we can afford. "Develop your business first before building your house" (Prov. 24:27). But all of us should carefully examine what kind of loans we qualify for and what our options are. We may be able to afford more than we think.

Banks and savings institutions are recognizing the price of housing and the fact a home is now a major investment. The rule of thumb used to be that banks discouraged home buyers from paying out more than 25 percent of their monthly income for housing. In recent years, though, I have seen banks and saving and loans approve loans for which the monthly payments represented as much as 40 percent of a family's after-tax income. This is logical, for the money that is spent for a home isn't lost; it is often returned with handsome profit when the property is sold.

Setting Limits—Lower or Higher

Deciding how much you can afford for a home, and then qualifying for a loan, requires some detailed planning. Let's look at some hypothetical scenarios.

In the first, let's assume that you are married, have three children and both you and your husband work. You have saved approximately $10,000, and have *risk* money in mutual funds. Your gross income, including any interest from savings or dividends, is $43,850. You have minimal deductions. All credit cards are paid off at the end of the month. Your car is financed through a credit union, yielding $650 in tax deductible interest, and you have contributions totalling $1200 per year, state withholding tax of $2,725 annually and $510 of miscellaneous expenses over the 2 percent AGI stipulated in current tax law. Your total deductions for itemizing consideration are $4,435. In order to do itemized deductions, a joint return needs $5,000 in total deductions. You are $565 short.

Deducting $9,750 for your personal exemptions (5 × 1,950), taxable income will be reduced to $34,100, leaving you with a federal obligation of $5,681. If you are required to pay state taxes, then your gross taxes will be greater and need to be determined for your state return separately.

Gross Income	$43,850
Personal Exemptions	−9,750
Taxable Income	$34,100
Federal Tax (1988)	$ 5,681

Since you don't own a home, let's assume your rental costs are $650 a month. On an annual basis, rent totals $7,800. Rent is not tax deductible. Some states do allow a renter's credit, usually quite small.

In scanning your newspaper, let's say you notice ads for a new development. Three bedroom homes are advertised for as little as 10 percent down with beginning prices of $92,500. Lenders are willing to do 90 percent financing if you meet their requirements. To qualify for a loan of $83,250 (92,500 - 9,250 = $83,250), you need to determine a few things. First, how much your monthly payment would be, then what effect a mortgage deduction would have on your taxes, and, if needed, can you handle any increases in housing expenses?

Qualifying with Lenders

Lenders have a variety of formulas when determining whether you qualify. One rule of thumb is to take your *gross* income and divide it by 12 to get an average monthly income before any taxes. Most lenders will allow 28 percent to 32 percent for fixed obligations and housing debts, car loans, etc. Some even allow a higher percentage. By multiplying your gross monthly income by these percentages, you can estimate an amount that a conservative lender would view as acceptable. The *etc.* I mentioned above refers to any other debt that shows up on your credit report. Most lenders estimate that outstanding revolving accounts (department stores, VISA, Mastercard) require a minimum payment of 5 percent of the balance. That minimum amount gets included in the 28 percent to 32 percent figure. In your case, you have no credit card debt, but do have a car payment.

In the second scenario, let's assume that all of the above holds true and you make an offer to buy the $92,500 home with 10 percent down. Your average income is $3,654 per month ($43,850 \div 12 = 3,654$). Twenty-eight percent of $3,654 is $1,023; 32 percent is $1,169. In this first step, you have determined that your safe range for combined housing and other debt obligations will be from $1,023 to $1,169 per month.

Step two now comes into play. A $83,250 mortgage at 11 percent amortized for 30 years would total $9,514 per year, or $793 a month. In estimating real estate taxes, I have used $1,000 a year. That amount will vary from state to state. Your total obligation would then be $10,514 annually, or $876 per month. So far so good.

Mortgage at 11%	$83,250
Mortgage payments	$ 9,514
Real estate taxes	1,000
Total	$10,514 ÷ 12
Monthly payment	$ 876

If you purchase a condominium or a co-op, there are usually ongoing monthly association dues. Make sure you add them in to your overall housing expenses within the 28 percent to 32 percent figure; the lender will.

Help, Uncle Sam

Now let's go back to our previous example, where there were not enough deductions to exceed the $5,000 minimum for the married filing jointly zero bracket. Mortgage interest and taxes are deductible. Let's assume that $115 of the $9,514 in mortgage payments is paid toward principal—shocking, isn't it? But, that's how payments work out the first few years of any loan for a home. Therefore, $9,399 in interest $(9,514 - 115 = 9,399)$ plus $1,000 in real estate taxes, creates a $10,399 additional deduction. Adding $10,399 to $4,435, your total gross deductions are now $14,834. This amount will be reduced by $5,000 (the standard deduction for a married couple filing jointly), giving an excess deduction of $9,834.

New deductions	$10,399
Old deductions	+4,435
	$14,834

Zero bracket for	
married filing jointly	–5,000
Excess deductions	$9,834

Now, adjust your gross income of $43,850 by your personal exemptions of $9,750 and $9,834 for excess deductions. Your taxable income declines to $24,266, leaving you with a revised federal tax obligation of $3,640.

Gross income	$43,850
Personal Exemptions	-9,750
Excess deductions	–9,834
	24,266

Federal tax	3,640

Deduct the new federal tax from your previous one of $5,681. Your total tax savings with the purchase of the house is $2,041 per year, or $170 a month. This does not take into consideration any tax savings on your state return.

Taxes pre-purchase	$5,681
Less new tax	-3,640
	$2,041 ÷ 12

Monthly savings	$170

If you purchase the home, take into consideration the tax savings and your current estimated rental obligation. You can allocate $850 per month without any change in your life-style. Since the monthly payment including taxes is $876 a month, there is a difference of only $26.

Rental for housing	$650
Tax savings	170
Purchase cost	-850
Total	($26)

Your next question should be, can you come up with that extra $26 each month? Ideally, the house should appreciate enough to cover any negative cash flow (as in your $60 a month), plus closing costs upon future sale.

These kinds of exercises will tell you, in exact terms, what kind of income you have, what kind of ongoing expenses you have, and what kind of funds are available to support the payment or purchase. With all this information you will be fully prepared to decide what kind and price of home you can afford.

My example was for a married couple with three children. If you are single, with or without children, or married with fewer or more children, the numbers still hold true. Use the tax tables in chapter 5 and determine where you are today, no matter how much you make or have saved. You need a starting point. This will give you one.

Tax Advantages

The tax advantages that go with home ownership have

been referred to in previous chapters. Basically, there are two types. One is deductions. You can deduct the interest on a mortgage loan. This amounts to more in the first few years of the loan, because the first years of payments apply primarily toward interest charges. You can also deduct the property and other taxes. Otherwise you'd be paying tax twice on the same money. Examples of this are outlined above.

Eventually you may decide to sell your home. Herein is another tax advantage. No matter what the appreciation has been, if you sell your house and buy another for at least as much money within 24 months, you defer any tax due on the gain. And, if you happen to be over the age of 55, you pay no taxes on realized profits up to $125,000, even if you don't choose to buy another house. You may want to sell and buy another home for any number of reasons. One reason may be simple ability and inclination to own a more valuable house. You could have a baby and need a larger home. Perhaps your children grew up, left, and you want a smaller home. Or, your home may need so much repair that it would be cheaper to buy another than repair the present one.

Some women cling to their homes like snails to their shell. Or they may hesitate because the thought of preparing a house for sale is so overwhelming. Don't let emotion or inertia keep you in a home you don't want or have outgrown. You can cope if you really try. Call a good Realtor whose advice you can trust, show her through the house and ask what needs to be done to make it marketable. Now is the time to think of your home objectively, not as a place you've put so much of yourself into, but as a piece of real estate to be displayed to its best advantage. You may find that your satisfaction at doing the job well more than compensates for lack of involvement in the home itself. Moving on can be profitable, both financially and emotionally.

To illustrate just how real estate becomes a good investment, turn back to the second half of chapter 6. In looking at credit, leverage was discussed, first in buying your own $100,000 home, then in buying four separate single family houses. These examples were very helpful in explaining profitable use of simple leverage, or credit. They are even more helpful in terms of ways and means to make money in real estate. The figures from chapter 6 do indeed tell a compelling story. In determining how, when, or even if, to buy and/or sell real estate, let the figures do the talking. You may be happily surprised at the outcome.

Some Rules of Thumb

First, make the smallest down payments possible. The less you have invested in property, the easier it may be for someone else to buy and the faster you can sell. This applies to your home as well as investment property. At times, buyers would rather assume a mortgage than get a new loan. Usually the existing mortgage has a better interest rate. And, by assuming the existing mortgage, a buyer can save certain closing costs—another advantage.

You ought to know by now that if it makes sense to use other people's money, you can and should. If you have more money going toward taxes than you can conceive of saving, then it may be possible to borrow your down payment. Of course, there are limits to this. You have to be sure that you can make the payments on the mortgage. You also need some back-up monies and established credit to qualify for these loans. Banks and savings and loan companies have their own formulas for determining how much debt they will allow a party to undertake. But the overall procedure is not substantially different from that outlined above, in which you determined your ability to take on a home mortgage.

If you are nearing retirement, then being in debt and leveraged should be avoided. This strategy only makes sense if you are paying taxes, have many years of paid work ahead and are comfortable with owning others' money.

Fixed or Variable?

Today's mortgage markets are complex. There are so many varieties of loans available: fixed, variable rate, combinations—15-, 30-, even 40-year loans. Fixed rate mortgages are old-fashioned, the kind your folks had. The interest rate and the monthly mortgage payment remain constant throughout the life of the mortgage. Variable rate mortgages adjust periodically to reflect changes in other interest rates or indexes in the economy.

Most borrowers prefer fixed rate mortgages. If interest rates go up, you don't care—your monthly mortgage payment stays at the same rate. If interest rates fall, you can refinance and get a lower rate mortgage. Sometimes there is a penalty, especially if refinancing is done within the first five years of when the loan originated.

Banks prefer variable rate mortgages. When interest rates rise, they must pay higher rates to depositors in order to be competitive with other financial institutions. This means they pay higher rates on savings and certificates of deposit. To pay the higher rates, they must get a greater return on their loaned monies—as in your mortgage. Banks are eager for borrowers to take out variable rate mortgages for just this reason. As a rule, all variable loans at origination carry interest rates that are several points lower than a fixed loan. It's a teaser, to get you in the door.

If you are debating which to take, determine if there is a *cap* on the loan. If there is, it is usually 5 percent. This means that if your loan began at 9 percent, it can increase to 14 percent. If a fixed loan is at 11 percent, it stays there. What does this mean in actual dollars? An 11 percent fixed 30-year loan for $100,000 is $915 per month. A 9 percent loan is $805—a difference of $110 per month, or $1,320 per year.

Most variable loans have a lifetime cap (5 percent) as well as an annual cap or a cap tied in to the particular index (6 month treasury bill, Federal District Funds, etc.). It could mean that although overall interest rates are up, yours may be up just a smidgen, because the annual cap keeps it from increasing significantly within a year's period. It could still be less than the fixed, at least for the first two to four years. What do you do? If you really plan to own this house for at least five years, go fixed. If you plan on selling within five years, then it doesn't matter which loan you choose. Ownership and loan rate decisions will be passed on to the next buyer. Never go with a variable rate that has no cap—interest rates can go sky-high.

Successful Selling

A good rule of thumb for selling decisions is (1) don't buy land that you have to resell in a hurry (land doesn't often sell when you want it to, and it is difficult to eat!) and (2), if you can sell your real estate and move on to something else, you are almost always better off. A corollary to this is buy property in the path of progress. If you are too far-sighted and buy property in the boondocks, you'll have to put it into your estate and pass it on to your heirs for it to do you any good.

Sell decisions, by the way, may be made for several reasons. In ideal circumstances, it is a decision where goals have been reached, benefits obtained and funds shall be put to use elsewhere.

Use a Professional

There is one more rule of thumb—use a real estate agent or broker. Looking on your own and answering ads in the newspaper may be a waste of your valuable time. You might stumble onto something, but more than likely, you won't. There are several reasons to use the professionals: time, money, information, skill—your time and money, his or her information and skill. Bargains are generally not found on every corner. Unlike the offers at K-Mart, there are no blue light specials.

Your agent should be knowledgeable about trends in the area you want, available to you for any questions, possess some tax savvy and not be so money-blinded that all he or she is interested in is closing the deal.

Discuss your specific needs, explaining your objectives and anticipated holding time. Let the agent know you are not a bottomless pit of money. There are, of course, no guarantees as to when you will sell—want to or be able to. Real estate can be slow. If you have to supplement any mortgage payment rent doesn't cover, you need cash to back it up. Then wait. Depending on what you told the agent your objectives were, it may take some time before a property appears that meets your criteria. Be patient. The best deals often take time to simmer.

Evaluating a Property

Some of the criteria listed here apply specifically to large rental complexes like apartment and commercial buildings. But there are some basic standards that should be applied to every purchase, steps to help ensure that you're getting what you pay for in a piece of real estate. In other words, to make your money work.

Try to establish the value of the property you're about to buy as closely as you can. Compare the price to the advertised prices of other similar properties in the same area. Hire a certified appraiser, if necessary, to inspect the property and judge its value.

Carefully examine the property and check its physical condition. If you are buying a single-family home, mentally eliminate all the furnishings of the present owner. They are not part of the deal. Ask yourself how the house will look without the furniture, rugs and pictures. Ask and then include in your written offer what appliances, if any, are to stay. When you are buying into a new development, don't take the word of the salespeople that sewers, water and gas lines, and paved roads will be constructed. Unfortunately, some will say anything to close a deal. Get it in writing as part of the contract, and if the developer is leery about making that legal commitment, then you ought to be leery of buying.

If you're buying a house, a duplex or triplex for rental income, find out what comparable homes in the area are renting for. (The classified ads in a daily newspaper will provide a guide.) Determine whether the rental income you expect, minus normal expenses, will be enough to cover the mortgage payments. If not, do you have excess cash to cover the shortage?

When it comes to buying into a major apartment complex, the process of evaluation is even more detailed. I rely on a long checklist before I will commit myself to purchase:

✔ What's happening in the rental housing market in that area, what's available and what rents are being charged. What kind of vacancies have the complex and surrounding area experienced?

✔ What kinds of tenants the apartment is likely to attract, with special attention to probable income level. It's important that tenants be compatible. That means similar ages and social backgrounds. You wouldn't want an apartment of two or three singles living next to a retired couple, for example.

✔ What are the profiles of the tenants already occupying the building: how well they've treated their unit and the building, how prompt they've been in paying their rent?

✔ What is the physical condition of the building and furnishings, if any? Plumbing and wiring are important, of course. You'll need to know whether there are any outstanding code violations that will have to be corrected. And replacing drapes and carpets can be expensive.

✔ What are the nature and status of the community surrounding the building? Does it seem to be prosperous and growing? A failing neighborhood will tend to drag a building down with it. If you plan to rent to families with children, are schools and churches nearby? The geographic location of the building can be important, too. A building near an ocean beach is subject to far more wear from the elements than an identical building two miles from shore.

✔ What current rents are being charged for each apartment or office, and how long have they stayed at that level? It would be difficult to raise rents immediately if they have recently been increased, though this dictum doesn't necessarily hold if the higher rent is accompanied by visible improvements to the property to make it cleaner, safer, more attractive. In fact, when tenants see an owner improving property, it almost creates a loyalty— they are willing to pay more.

✔ What is the gross multiplier of the area? This figure is the ratio of the price of the building to the annual gross income it brings. It's fairly uniform in any given community, and it varies according to the affluence of the area and the demand and availability of rental housing. Any agent working in the commercial area (buildings, apartments) will know multipliers without blinking an eye.

In the area where my office is located, Palo Alto, California, the gross multiplier ranges from 12 to 15. That is, the value of the apartments could be 12 to 15 times greater than the annual rental income. This is due to the value of the land, the limited housing available and the general prosperity of the area. In an undesirable area, the same apartment house might have a multiplier of no more than two. You could, theoretically, pay off the price of the building with two year's rent. That doesn't mean that this property is a better deal, however. There are reasons why the price is so low compared to the income received.

One of my clients purchased a bargain property in a depressed neighborhood. Eventually, he walked away, deeding the apartment to the city rather than pay the huge heating bill and legal expenses incurred in dealing with a tenant group that cared very little about the condition of the property.

You also need to check:

✔ The lot size and legal description (this applies to any property you're thinking of buying).

✔ Any rights-of-way or encroachments that might prevent you from adding on to property or adding improvements like a patio or swimming pool.

✔ The availability of on-street parking if a parking lot is not included with the property.

✔ The possible maintenance costs of swimming pools, patios, gardens, new roofs and the like.

✔ A few years ago, condominiums were the vogue, especially for second homes, which were then rented out. Vogues pass. Make sure you note trends and whether there could be a glut on the horizon.

✔ If the building has an elevator, what condition is it in? In California, any commercial building over two stories high must have an elevator. What rules and codes are there in your state?

✔ Everyone needs utilities. Who pays for them? If it's you, the landlord, make sure you check at least one year's previous bills.

✔ The age of the building, and the length of time since the last major renovations.

The National Institute of Real Estate Management has a guideline for expenses that an owner should expect, expressed in percentages of the gross income, and broken down as to states and specific cities. With few exceptions, it is an excellent source for all properties, ranging from duplexes to huge apartments. Guidelines include percentages for management fees, legal and accounting, utilities, real estate taxes, upkeep, painting and gardening, overall maintenance, insurance, wiring, roofing and plumbing. Remember these percentages may vary, though the total comes to 40 to 45 percent for ongoing expenses. The remainder would be available for debt service, establishing a reserve fund for funding expenses or cash flow.

SINGLE-FAMILY HOMES

There are many types of real estate to invest in, one of which is the single-family home.

If you have an eye for turning ugly ducklings into swans, look for the junker on the block, maybe the least attractive home in the immediate area, and make a low offer to the seller.

Some people buy homes to rent out. The tenant in turn makes most, if not all, of the mortgage payments during the ownership period. I can remember clients who started with one house, purchased another and now have strings of ten or fifteen homes. They've turned this into a vocation, a full-time business, eventually quitting their former jobs.

Anyone who bought property in the '70s made a fortune. The turbulent interest rates of the '80s slowed down the appreciation potential, sobering the marketplace somewhat. Although I don't expect to see triple and quadruple values in real estate as created in the past, I do feel there are still plenty of opportunities. The key is to invest smart. You'll simply have to be more careful and more selective than would have been necessary a few years ago.

Look for areas that haven't yet experienced the boom that recently swept through California and Boston, for example. At one time, Houston and Dallas, Texas, were great spots. That was until the cost of oil plummeted. Last year, developers were actually knocking down apartment buildings in Texas—the market glut in action.

Check areas where manufacturing and industrial firms may be relocating, places that seem on the brink of major growth. The general idea is to look for cities where the living is less expensive than in the big cities, where city and county government is friendly to growth and new industry, where state laws—as in Nevada—give a tax break to relocating corporations. Consider areas that have energy resources. Those are the very elements that companies seek when they're looking for a place to locate a plant. Where there is a big plant, there will be jobs, and that will mean an influx of workers and a demand for housing.

FIXER-UPPERS

If you have an eye for turning ugly ducklings into swans, look for the junker on the block, maybe the least attractive home in the immediate area, and make a low offer to the seller. The idea is to get the price you will pay as far below the prevailing standard of the neighborhood as possible, then clean and paint and generally tidy up the place before immediately putting it back on the market.

It's amazing what a fresh coat of paint, a few day's worth of cleaning, and $100 in garden plants will do for the value of a home. Appraisers seem to love the orderliness and color that plants bring to a home. I've seen a few newly planted petunias make a difference of $5,000 in two appraisers' estimates of the value of a home that otherwise was exactly the same as it had been. "Curb appeal" is one of the most important impressions when a potential buyer gets out of the car. The kitchen and bathrooms are next.

HELLO, UNCLE SAM

When it comes time to sell and you have a gain, hopefully a hefty one, you can defer the tax consequences. How? By buying another property and having the new purchase close escrow on the same day as the house you sold. Escrow, which completes all the paperwork of any transaction in real estate, is usually handled by a third party, independent of the buyer and seller, as well as their respective agents. Assuming the new purchase costs more than the sale, the IRS will allow you to defer any taxation until you sell again at a later date. If the new property costs less than the other, then you will have some tax due. You do not have the luxury of a 24-month wait as you do with your personal residence.

Federal income tax laws make a specific differentiation between personal property and property bought to produce income. With multiple-unit buildings such as duplexes, triplexes or apartments, the portion in square footage used by a live-in owner is regarded as personal property, while the remaining percentage is treated as income property.

It's possible to change the character of property from personal to income by renting the house for at least six months. Widows or divorcées who own a large home that is too expensive in upkeep may want to consider moving out, renting or buying another, and renting their own to someone else for at least half a year. They get all the tax advantages of owning income property (primarily depreciation), and then they can sell the house and trade up to a duplex or small apartment. When a property is traded or exchanged, the taxable gain is deferred. Now, if you are over 55, this strategy may be inappropriate. The $125,000 one-time-only gain is allowed on personal residences only. If you find yourself in this situation, make sure you talk to your tax advisor before making any commitments.

BEING A LANDLORD IS NOT EASY

The drawback to having income property is that acting as a landlord isn't for everybody. It isn't profitable, for one thing, to attempt to keep your rental property the most charming house on the street. That isn't to say it shouldn't be clean, neat and safe, but your tenants probably won't be as careful of the house's appearance as you are. Forget about the *Better Homes and Gardens* look—it's a losing battle with tenants. If it would seriously bother you to own property that just isn't perfect, then maybe being a landlord isn't for you.

Even tougher is the fact that renting a home, or a series of homes, is a business and has to be approached as such. This means there are times when you'll have to do things that may come hard for you—like pestering tenants who have fallen behind on their rent and even evicting those who mistreat the property or are seriously in arrears with their rent. Even raising rents can be difficult.

One alternative to being a landlord is to get into another phase of real estate—renovating. This is buying, fixing up and then reselling and never dealing with renters.

Another is to hire a management firm that will, for a percentage of the rent, assume such duties as interviewing prospective tenants, collecting rent, arranging for routine and extraordinary maintenance (the cost of which the landlord will bear), keeping track of the house's condition and evicting any tenants who fail to live up to the terms of the rental agreement.

These management firms are available for every type of property. Most specialize in one type or another, so do a little legwork before you decide which firm to hire. Call companies you see listed in the Yellow Pages and interview several that specialize in the kind of housing in which you have invested. Contact the local Chamber of Commerce and ask if there is an apartment or commercial building association in the area. Most large cities have them. Most put out a magazine for members; ask for a sample copy. There will be ads galore. Compare their prices and services. Make sure the company is experienced. Ask for references and then *check* them. That means calling the owners of other properties and maybe even driving to visit those properties, to see whether they are well maintained and clean.

You will save a good deal of money if you can manage the place yourself. But it's money that you will *earn*. As the landlord, you are responsible for the condition of the property. That means you or your estate manager must be handy at minor plumbing, electrical and carpentry jobs. You must know when to give up and call an expert. And you have to be ready to come to the rescue at almost any time. Calls for help can come at any hour, any day, any night.

In today's society, lawsuits seem to ooze out of the woodwork. Don't skimp on insurance coverage. For less than $200, you can get a rider on your policy that can cover what's called "hurt feelings" for up to $1 million. It's kind of a catch-all clause.

BEING YOUR OWN AGENT

Many of the same considerations apply to selling a house yourself. Undeniably, there is much money to be saved—$6,000 to $7,000 in commissions on the sale of a $100,000 house. I mentioned earlier that you should deal with an agent—someone who can market your property. If you happen to be someone who can do the job effectively, then it may be worth a try. This includes being able to write an attractive advertisement for the newspapers, being able to show the house and follow up on telephone inquiries from prospective buyers at all times, including evenings and weekends.

You must know the current state of the money market in your area—who is lending how much money at what percentage rate—so that you can steer buyers toward the right lending institution. It means understanding the workings of title companies and escrow companies and banks, and understanding how to fill out contracts and deposit forms. Your time is usually more valuable than you think. Dozens, even hundreds, of hours will be devoted to the job of selling before you are finally successful. Personally, I prefer to get the exposure of a multiple listing service and let somebody else earn the commission.

MULTI-UNIT HOMES

Into this category I put duplexes, triplexes, four-plexes, even six-plexes, anything between a single-family home and a typical apartment house. Though most of what I've said about single-family homes as rentals applies as well to these buildings, multi-unit housing offers the owner the choice of living in one of the units while collecting rent that may well cover the entire mortgage payment.

Generally, these buildings feature an owner's unit that is somewhat bigger and nicer than the others. If you choose not to use it yourself, its features will usually fetch a higher rent than those of the other units. Should you decide to live on the premises, you'll find it necessary for tax purposes to compute the total square footage of the building and to find what percentage of the floor area the owner's unit comprises. Again, it's advisable to get tax help here.

APARTMENTS

Apartment buildings can range from large converted homes with six or eight private rooms to multibuilding complexes with hundreds of units. Not many are able to start their investment in real estate by purchasing a huge apartment complex. Most, in fact, should not start that way. But I will note that the greater the number of units, the greater the chances of the gross income's covering expenses and mortgage payments. The chances of having a negative cash flow increase with fewer units. Owners of such buildings often have to supplement the rental income with funds from some outside source. When it's time to sell, agents' fees and commissions become quite negotiable with larger apartment buildings and complexes, often less than the standard 6 percent of the sales price. At the other end of the scale, commissions tend to be firm.

When buying an apartment, make sure you get professional help before signing on any dotted line—both in tax advice, as well as possible management help. There are numerous pitfalls both in the buying and the running of such buildings. Most cities and states require an on-site manager for buildings with sixteen or more units.

COMMERCIAL COMPLEXES

Some of the developments represented here constitute the upper end of the real estate investment spectrum. Shopping malls and downtown office buildings are well beyond the reach of most of us, at least as single investors. But much of the thinking that goes into such projects can be applied to smaller ventures as well.

Walk into any modern shopping mall and you'll notice that the shopping center is dominated by two or three major stores—Safeway, perhaps, or Macys, Sears or J.C. Penney. They are known as "anchor tenants" for the project. They serve a number of purposes.

Usually the anchor tenants are the first committed to the mall, often before any construction begins. These companies sign long leases, providing security for the builders and the owners. Most are triple net leases, leases that include stipulations that rent is to increase automatically as taxes, utilities and the cost of living. Major tenants then attract the smaller stores, who hope to take advantage of the heavy foot traffic the big stores generate.

These big deals are far beyond the reach of most of us. If available to private investors, they will more than likely be packaged in the form of a limited partnership. Partnerships often have thousands of other partners who usually invest a minimum of $5,000. There are pros and cons to these, as you will discover later in this book.

Before leaving this chapter, let me reiterate the value of professional assistance. The financiers who put huge shopping malls together wouldn't dream of doing so without specialized, experienced lawyers and accountants. There's no reason why you should treat your investments, especially in the area of real estate, any differently.

Proverbs 12:11 forewarns, "He who works his land will have abundant food, but he who chases fantasies lacks judgment" *(NIV)*. Exercise your judgment by doing your homework. Don't be afraid to follow your dreams, but if they are clouded, then avoid the deal. There will always be another.

CHAPTER THIRTEEN
Limited Partnerships— Pooling Funds

A limited partnership is a pooling of funds for investment purposes, offering the investor a passive role while a general partner manages the investment. Also known as syndications, limited partnerships can offer the investor an opportunity to buy part of a very large commercial complex, shopping center or apartment building that would be difficult, if not impossible, to purchase as an individual.

The person or company who organizes a partnership acts as general partner and retains responsibility for managing, selecting and selling the partnership property. The limited, or passive, partners, do not participate in the decisions and thus do not bear liability for bank loans or contract the general partner may enter into on behalf of the partnership. Limited partnerships are supposed to relieve an investor of the burden of management and day-to-day operations. In addition, if all goes well, they offer a combination of income, appreciation and some tax shelter.

On paper, this sounds like an ideal situation for the smaller investor who wants to be in "real estate," but cannot do it alone. The ingredients are there for success. Indeed, during the 1970s, limited partnerships made excellent investments with particular appeal to women. But today the story is different. The unfolding realities of cumbersome management, changing security and tax laws, conflicting information and IRS scrutiny, often mean

---

It is advisable to have an attorney or advisor read and interpret any prospectus for you, especially if you are a novice or feel unsure.

---

that limited partnerships yield only unlimited grief. More than most investments, this one requires caution. "Don't go to war without wise guidance; there is safety in many counselors," warns Proverbs 24:6. Many invest in limited partnerships for tax benefits—they are at war with the IRS.

WHAT INVESTMENT SHOULD YOU CONSIDER?

Limited partnerships participate in a pot-pourri of areas: oil and gas, hotels, public storage, equipment, agriculture, research and development, shopping malls, cattle ranches, fast food outlets—you name it, someone has syndicated and sold it.

Americans invested billions of dollars in public real estate limited partnerships throughout the '80s. Because most private partnerships are not registered with the Securities and Exchange Commission, there is no way to gauge the total sums placed. It is estimated public offerings represent only the tip of the iceberg, and the funds going into private partnerships are many times the amount placed in public offerings.

You do have the protection of a partnership prospectus, but this is first and foremost a legal document, often written in legalese, without anywhere near the information available from major stock exchange issuings or publicly traded mutual funds. A prospectus may contain little straightforward information about the actual investments of the partnership or its probability in achieving profit goals. It is advisable to have an attorney or advisor read and interpret any prospectus for you, especially if you are a novice or feel unsure.

CONSIDER YOUR INVESTMENT PARTNERS

Because a limited partnership gives much exclusive power to the general partner, it's important you consider the size and expertise of your fellow investors. It's not only the idea of the partnership that counts, it's what the people who organize them do with the investments. The Bible encourages us to join with others, to take counsel and work together. But it also warns us to know our counsellors: "Putting confidence in an unreliable man is like chewing with a sore tooth, or trying to run on a broken foot" (Prov. 25:19). In fact, 2 Chronicles 20:37 is even more explicit about aligning ourselves with the wrong people:

> Then Eliezer, son of Dodavahu from Mareshah, prophesied against Jehoshaphat, telling him, "Because you have allied yourself with King Ahaziah, the Lord has destroyed your work." So the ships met disaster and never arrived at Tarshish.

The size of limited partnerships often makes it difficult to heed the warnings of the Bible. Investments in partnerships come in two major forms: public limited partnerships and private limited partnerships. The primary differences include the number of investors involved. As a rule, private offerings will have fewer than 35 limited partners; public offerings can have from 35 to over 4,000 partners. One way to protect yourself as to the reliability and legality of a partnership is to ask some specific questions about its objectives and operation. Some of these questions are listed at the end of this chapter.

MORE SPECIFICS ABOUT PARTNERSHIPS

Within a limited partnership, all income tax benefits and losses flow directly to the partners. The partnership itself is a reporting entity and is not taxed as a corporation would be.

Because private syndications have fewer investors, the amount of funds invested are often in excess of $20,000 per partner. On the other hand, in public syndications, participation can be as low as $2,000 per investor. Public partnerships often involve front-end fees that could amount to as much as 35 percent of the actual dollars raised. Private partnerships often place anywhere from 80 percent to 95 percent into the actual properties purchased, but that's not guaranteed. There are gougers out there. Make sure you read the small print, especially the section that details how the monies raised are to be used. If that's not listed in the prospectus, toss it—there's always another deal.

General partners receive their compensation in a number of ways: when the property is purchased, front-end fees, ongoing management fees and a share of the profits when the property is sold. These are usually identified as "substantial fees." Know up front who gets what, when and how.

MASTER LIMITED PARTNERSHIPS

Conceived in 1981, master limited partnerships have gained plenty of attention since the far-reaching Tax Reform Act of 1986 was implemented.

In a nutshell, they are quite similar to limited partnerships, except they are traded on a major stock exchange. Limited partnerships are not liquid investments. There is some selling of units with the help of the syndicator or general partner, or a group specifically designed for repurchase of already existing limited partnership units. But, there's a catch: The repurchase is often at a substantial discount from what you originally paid.

Any income derived from a master limited partnership is taxed at your regular tax rate. Many corporations have converted to master limited partnerships to take advantage of the lower tax rates for individuals. Of course, if there is an increase in tax rates again, this trend will stop abruptly.

PASSIVE VERSUS ACTIVE

The tax codes continue to affect both limited partnerships and master limited partnerships. Under present law, they can be used to offset passive losses including those from older partnerships. If a taxable distribution is generated in a master limited partnership, the older, loss-producing tax shelters can be used as an offset. There is a catch—if you

purchase a master limited partnership that owns mortgages, any income produced will be considered investment income, not passive income. Passive income is
needed to offset passive losses. You might want to refer
back to Passive Income and Losses in chapter 5.

Through 1990, some deduction of losses generated
from partnerships that originated before October 22,
1986, will be allowed, but only on a declining basis: In
1988, 35 percent of the loss is allowed as a deduction, 20
percent in 1989 and 10 percent in 1990.

Tax shelters have long been a major benefit of the limited partnership. But tax reforms have reduced, and in
some places eliminated, the lure of most partnerships.
Many were sold with the primary carrot of tax breaks and
paper losses. The latter part of the '80s popularized partnerships that emphasized income—unheard of in the early
'80s, when all anyone really sought were deductions.
Times are changing, and the IRS is looking very critically
at all abusive or questionable shelters. For instance, IRS
now requires all limited partnerships to be registered in
advance.

INVESTIGATE BEFORE INVESTING

If you do decide the potential benefits of a limited partnership outweigh the risks and inconveniences, there are a
few guidelines that will increase your probabilities of success. Make sure you do the following, for "the man who
strays away from common sense will end up dead!" (Prov.
21:16).

✔ Check on the background and experience of the
syndicators and general partner of the partnership. Ask
for a financial statement and references. Bear in mind that

a limited partnership is a nonliquid investment. Invest through large brokerage houses or investment companies. They don't necessarily offer the best deals, but if they do mislead you, at least there will be someone around to hold accountable should the deal go sour.

✔ Make sure your objectives are the same as the partnership's—to produce ongoing monthly income, to gain significant tax deductions, growth, etc.

✔ Ask whether the property(s) will be obtained through a blind pool or if it has already been selected. If possible, visit the property. Blind pool means they decide and purchase after the monies are raised.

✔ Avoid partnerships that have upfront fees and charges of more than 20 percent.

✔ Verify who gets paid first when the property is sold—the limited partners or the general partner? Don't get involved if the general partner gets funds before the limited partners.

✔ Avoid partnerships that borrow money through zero-coupon mortgages. Any gains can be eaten up by deferred interest when assets are sold.

✔ Read the prospectus—all of it. Have your accountant, tax advisor, attorney or financial planner review it before you commit yourself. Objectives should always be clearly identified.

✔ Spread the risk. If you want to put $15,000 into partnerships, buy $5,000 in three different partnerships, preferably in three different businesses. This may limit your choices because many partnerships require higher minimum investments. It may also mean more time and energy in initial research. But it will give you the advantage of diversification as well as a variety of experience with which to weigh future investment decisions.

✔ Be conservative on taxes. Avoid partnerships that offer more than 100 percent of your investment in tax deductions. That will eliminate most of the deals that are outright frauds and will probably keep the IRS at bay.

✔ Buy only if it makes economic sense. Don't ever buy for tax losses.

✔ Finally, be aware that a limited partnership is *Caveat Emptor:* Buyer Beware. There is money to be made. But if it sounds "too good to be true," then it probably is. Heed Proverbs 24:32-34:

> Then, as I looked, I learned this lesson:
> "A little extra sleep,
> A little more slumber,
> A little folding of the hands to rest"
> means that poverty will break in upon you suddenly like a robber, and violently like a bandit.

Nothing is guaranteed. Most people who made investments in limited partnerships in the early '80s have not fared well. The laws have changed, the economy and environment have changed, and the odds are, you have changed, too.

Time has shown that limited partnerships have minimal flexibility—something coveted and sought after in today's financial world.

Be cautious—two appropriate words for exiting this chapter.

CHAPTER FOURTEEN
Collecting for Fun *and* Profit

We all collect things. Things as simple as photographs, as whimsical as comic books, as complex as jewelry, or as valuable as gold and silver. Women in particular have traditionally taken great joy in collectibles—their beauty, their nostalgic connection with the past, the security, as well as the delight and pride in having something tangible and treasured. "Women," says novelist Eudora Welty in *The Ponder Heart,* "see human thought and feeling best and clearest by seeing it through something solid."[1] So our affinity for collectibles comes naturally.

Christians, too, have a natural appreciation for earthly goods. From the days of Moses, material goods have been enjoyed. "They brought to the Lord their offerings of gold, jewelry—earrings, rings from their fingers, necklaces—

and gold objects of every kind" (Exod. 35:22).

Even the Wise Men brought collectibles to honor Jesus: "Then they opened their presents and gave him gold, frankincense and myrrh" (Matt. 2:11). We are all aware of Jesus' warning to: "Watch out! Be on your guard against all kinds of greed; a man's life does not consist in the abundance of his possessions," shares Luke 12:15 *(NIV)*. But there's no reason life cannot be enhanced by possessions.

As long as you don't need to get your cash out in a hurry, collectibles can be good long-term, anti-inflation investments.

ASSESSING FINANCIAL VALUE

If you love collecting things, there's no reason your hobby cannot have financial, as well as aesthetic, value. Collectibles, of course, cannot be considered a major investment strategy, for they are, in fact, the most illiquid of investments. Their value depends not only on the economy and market conditions, but also on your finding a willing buyer—someone who loves your collection as much or more than you do. Any quick cash sale will be at great discount. I remember selling some jewelry a few years ago, pieces that had some bad memories attached to them and pieces I no longer loved. I was shocked at the final sales price. It was 25 percent of what my insurance appraisal had been!

As long as you don't need to get your cash out in a

hurry, collectibles can be good long-term, anti-inflation investments. Despite my experience with the jewelry, I'm not turned off on collectibles; they can increase in value at a surprising rate. A friend of mine inherited her father's old electric trains and began adding to the set on her own. She was very casual about her "choo-choos," until an insurance agent suggested that a special rider with a $30,000 valuation would be only a modest protection for her collection. She had no idea other people valued old trains as much as she and her father did.

Over the last decade, items such as clocks, Tiffany lamps, English desks and Chinese porcelains have all appreciated many times over their original purchase price. It's true that in the recession of 1981 and 1982, several of the collectible areas, including gems, declined substantially in overall value. But such a decline allows an astute investor to add to her investments at bargain rates.

When you are considering collectibles, I suggest you do not include them in your net worth statement as long as they remain under 10 percent of the total value of your other assets. If their value is higher than 10 percent, they become material and are included with other investments on the net worth statement. It is also noteworthy that collectibles usually arise out of the interests of one marriage partner and therefore should be considered the separate property of that partner. If you began a jewelry collection with some baubles from your Aunt Martha's attic, they are yours alone.

SMART ITEMS TO COLLECT

If you do enjoy collecting, start to pay attention to ways you can make it successful as well as enjoyable. Items that are unusual, with historic value, are a good bet, especially items geared to kids. Since children are notoriously care-less with belongings, old toys and books in good condition are quite valuable. A single 1910 Pittsburgh Pirates Honus Wagner baseball card is worth $25,000; a 1938 *Superman* comic book is also worth $25,000.

Dolls

Doll collections are a natural. Many times I've said, "If only I had kept my old Madame Alexander dolls." Their value is right up there with older dolls made of antique por-celain. Price tags ranging from $200 to $7,000 are assigned to Shrader China dolls and Gorham's Colette dolls. Already Barbie and Ken dolls are becoming collector items, and original Cabbage Patch dolls sell for many times the original price. If you have young children, do them a favor and save any dolls that are in good condition. The value is significantly enhanced if the box is saved as well.

Recordings

Many recordings have good collection value. If you are a record buff, consider that an original Beatles 45 that sold in 1960 for $1 is now worth more than $30. The soundtrack of the 1966 James Bond movie, *Casino Royale,* is now out of print. If you can get one, its current value is about $75. Or, if you find any of the special promotional records dis-tributed to deejays prior to distribution of an album, you probably have something worth thousands of dollars. Besides availability, a record's condition will be the pri-mary benchmark of its value, and if it still has the jacket or paper sleeve it came in, even better.

Plates and Figurines

Plates and figurines have also long been popular. Hummel and Lladro figurines, as well as the Lennox Wildlife Collection of Animals in the Wild, are all cherished by collectors primarily because they are dated and limited. In 1978, a limited edition piece commemorating *Gone with the Wind*—the book and the movie—sold for $21.50 a plate. Less than 10 years later, each plate is worth approximately $200.

Glass

Another rule of thumb in collecting is to specialize, to concentrate on a specific subject or artist or period. Otherwise, you'll just accumulate, never really coming up with a defined collection. A friend of mine loves glassware—blown glass, cut glass, pressed glass. But because she had limited resources, she restricted her collecting to pressed glass. Not only did this help her curb impulse buying, it let her learn a lot about a narrow area and develop an admirable, complete and valuable collection of pressed glass.

Stamps and Coins

Stamps and coins can be good investments, but like everything else, they require study. These are probably collected more than any other items, but only quality and specific issues have increased appreciably in value. Catalogs will give an estimate of what a stamp or coin should bring to a dealer offering it for sale. If you use catalog prices to trade with a fellow collector, then both parties are using the same yardstick. But if you want to sell for cash, it's a different matter. Some real rarities may be snapped up well above the listed prices, while some items in plentiful supply may be almost impossible to move at any price. If you want to collect stamps or coins, join a philatelic or numismatic club, respectively, and do a lot of listening to experienced members before seriously considering your hobby as an investment.

Antique Furniture

An area of collecting where, with care and study, you may profit is antique furniture. There's generally a good market for furniture in case you ever have to sell, and it's easy to begin with a single item. Even if it's not expensive, one terrific piece will be likely to appreciate at a far greater rate than several ordinary ones. Buy conservatively, and stay away from speculative or fad items such as jukeboxes or slot machines. It makes sense to develop friendships with dealers for both information and for sources in finding pieces you might not locate on your own.

Art

An area of collecting where, even with care and study, you may not profit is art. This is a risky area unless you are buying masterpieces. If you know art, you may be able to pick a winner among unknown artists, but don't rely on the word of a gallery owner that an artist will be famous "someday." Better to collect an artist who is already acclaimed, even if it's only a signed print or limited lithograph. This art is more likely to go up in value, but even then, it's hard to find buyers. If you are interested in art, it's best to buy art that you enjoy; enjoyment may be all you ever get out of it.

The cash value for jewelry can fall far below its appraised value, so take advantage of the opportunity to wear and enjoy your investment while you own it.

Gems and Jewelry

A final area of collectibles worth considering is gemstones and jewelry. This happens to be a weakness of mine, but I'm the first to admit it is definitely a buyer-beware market. Much of the value of old jewelry these days is in the history, uniqueness and setting of the piece, or how it exemplifies one of the five major periods of estate jewelry. Avoid auction houses or fancy jewelers. You can find plenty of estate jewelry in small shops or at garage sales and flea markets for under $50.

As with art, it's important to buy jewelry you like. I have already given an example of how the cash value for jewelry can fall far below its appraised value, so take advantage of the opportunity to wear and enjoy your investment while you own it. The market for semi-precious gems is even more complicated than for jewelry. If you buy a stone, then set it in jewelry, you may actually decrease its value.

There are four areas to consider in purchasing gems: color, clarity, carat weight and cut. You should be able to evaluate each of these qualities before buying, and even then, you should have your intended purchase checked by a certified gemologist as to its authenticity. As with other collectibles, gems are long-term investments.

HOW GOLD AND SILVER FIT IN

If you're interested in collectibles, you have probably wondered by now about gold and silver. As we have seen, gold and silver have been recognized as symbols of wealth since biblical times. Does that still hold today? Does it still make sense for us to own gold and silver? The answer is yes, under certain circumstances. Metals can be a prudent investment at the right time and in the proper form and quantity.

Gold and silver fall into much the same category as semi-precious gems, except that the market for metals is more structured, the demand, easier to predict. They are collectibles in that they are investments in tangible forms of wealth that can provide an effective hedge against inflation. When the value of the dollar goes down, the value of precious metals often goes up. While it's not in everyone's interest to buy precious metals, there's a solid case for limited holdings as part of a diversification program. If your net worth exceeds $100,000, it is probably appropriate that about 10 percent of that be in gold or silver.

Gold

Like any collectible, it's important to be knowledgeable before investing in gold. Accumulated reserves of this virtually indestructible metal far exceed current output, so decisions to sell gold from existing stocks can have more impact on price than the ebb and flow of production. And since the primary use for gold is as a store of value (and much of it is stored by government), there is no simple way to analyze demand. What people will pay for gold is largely based on what they think other people will pay for gold in the future. Gold can be bought in several ways, but every method entails either a premium, a storage fee or an appraisal fee. One means is to buy gold coins like the Canadian Maple Leaf or the Austrian Kroner. You'll pay a premium for handling that will put the price somewhat above the actual value of the coin's weight in gold. Banks generally charge the lowest premium over gold content value, small coin shops the highest. Deak-Perera, a very large bullion dealer in New York, usually has good prices and can give you a price quote for comparison with local dealers. Remember, nearly all states charge taxes on sales of most gold coins.

Gold can also be purchased in solid pieces, from banks, full-service brokerage houses or from big bullion dealers. You can possess the actual gold, where you can actually stare at it and touch it. Or, you can accept a gold certificate that proves your ownership while the bars stay in a vault. Besides not having to store and insure the gold yourself, a big advantage of the certificate over the blocks or coins is lower trading costs.

Silver

Silver is far more plentiful than gold and is much less expensive, but it offers the same opportunities in the form of coins, bars and commodity contracts. Although governments own relatively little silver, it is still viewed as a store of value, a hard-money alternative to currency. And like gold, it has special industrial uses that are irreplaceable with any other metal. Thus, the economics and strategies of silver are similar to gold.

In the end, then, collectibles, including gold and silver, can have a place in your financial planning. But collectibles in particular should be considered as investments in the quality or enjoyment of your life, not as primary profit-making investments. It is true, as Proverbs 8:19 says, that the gifts of wisdom "are better than the purest gold or sterling silver," but with cautious, enthusiastic, prudent investment in collectibles, there is no reason you cannot have both.

Note
1. Eudora Welty, *The Ponder Heart* (San Diego: HarBraceJ, 1967).

CHAPTER FIFTEEN

Annuities—Not Just Another Gimmick!

Planning for the future is an important part of Christian stewardship. "There are four things that are small but unusually wise," says Proverbs 30:24. The first of these is, "Ants: they aren't strong, but store up food for the winter." Proper planting, growing and harvesting of selected investments will offer you security and freedom in your future. But there's another investment specifically geared for future years you may wish to consider.

Men are prone to think of retirement pensions and Social Security as sufficient means to ensure income after their working years. Women are more apt to realize that one's working years never really cease, for we work for God, our families, or for better quality of life *throughout* our lives. Pensions and Social Security are no guarantees of a secure financial future. Annuities, however, can offer some attractive guarantees, particularly for women.

Looking back to when I was a stockbroker and financial planner, I urged every one of my clients to purchase an annuity. Anyone who did thinks I'm a hero. High rates of return have been received, money is accessible and taxes have been deferred. Sound ideal? For many it was, and still is.

Annuities are uncomplicated—they are contracts with insurance companies. And you need to know the pros and cons to determine if they belong in your overall financial plan.

DEFERRED VS. NON

There are two types of annuity: the deferred and the immediate. Deferred literally means later—your money will accumulate interest during the deferral period. At a later date, you make the decision on how you want it: in a lump sum, annually, monthly or some other option. It is also known as a TDA (tax deferred annuity). The immediate annuity starts paying right away—the next month. This would normally be attractive to a woman who is in her later years and wants income now. Both types are purchased with after-tax dollars.

If your Aunt Martha gifts you with $15,000 and you feel an enormous stewardship toward the money, this may be your cup of tea.

PRE-TAX DOLLARS

There is another annuity known as the tax sheltered annuity, or TSA. Participants include teachers, certain government employees and those who work for tax-exempt organizations.

A TSA allows participants to direct a portion of their earnings, before taxes are withheld, to a special fund each year. At the end of the year, their W-2s reflect a lesser amount for tax reporting. Let's say you are a teacher and earn $23,000 a year. You decide to place $500 a month, or $6,000 a year, in a TSA. At the end of the year, your tax-

---

Investing in an annuity usually involves conservative, safe monies.

---

able income will be $17,000. Any federal and state taxes are deferred until you withdraw your funds at a later date. There is a catch, though. Social Security taxes are figured on the entire amount.

The only comparison would be the 401(k) plans that many corporations offer to their employees. With a TSA, an employee can contribute up to $9,500 of her annual income. With a 401(k) plan, the employee contributions are limited to $7,000.

CAN MONEY LAST FOREVER?

Investing in an annuity usually involves conservative, safe monies. In placing your money, it's a good idea to attempt to find out how long it will last after you have accumulated a specific amount or you have a lump sum to start with.

Under normal circumstances, we don't know how long we are going to live. You can, though, determine how much you can withdraw each year after you have accumulated some funds.

Remember Aunt Martha's $15,000? Let's say you are now 34 years old and with that $15,000 you purchased a TDA that has guaranteed interest for a period of 31 years at 10 percent. Insurance companies normally guarantee a high rate for the first few years, then drop the guarantee to 4 percent for the remainder of the deferral period. (My example will keep the rate constant.) Should you panic? No. Insurance companies have legal requirements stipulating they set assets aside to protect contract holders. Interest rates are usually lowballed for an extended period because of these requirements. Logic is needed here. If 10 years go by and they offer you a 4 percent return at renewal and the current market shows 9 percent, do you think you or anyone else would keep funds with them? No one in their right mind would. Insurance companies are forced to be current by competition and supply and demand.

Your $15,000 has earned interest at 10 percent for a period of 31 years. The size of your mini estate has grown to $287,915! Unbelievable, isn't it? It's often hard to grasp just how fast a dollar can grow if it's allowed to compound and you defer paying any taxes on interest or gains. Try it, you might like what it does to your pocketbook.

The following table will help you determine how long

How Long Will Your Money Last?

Number of years	6%	7%	8%	10%	12%
1	0.9434	0.9346	0.9259	0.9091	0.8929
5	4.2124	4.1002	3.9927	3.7908	3.6048
10	7.3601	7.0236	6.7101	6.1446	5.6502
15	9.7005	9.0900	8.5478	7.5952	6.8011
20	11.4699	10.5940	9.8181	8.5136	7.4694
25	12.7834	11.6536	10.6748	9.0770	7.8431
30	13.7648	12.4090	11.2578	9.4269	8.0552

your money will last. You have to provide the number of years over which you want to spread the withdrawal, as well as the annual interest rate you will earn.

The column on the left represents the number of years to withdraw. The percentages across the top are the interest rates you will continue to earn. At the point where the two intersect, divide the amount you have saved by the number you get. You now know how many years your nest egg will spread out.

Let's take your $287,915. You have decided that you want the money to last or payout to you over the next 25 years. Being conservative, you have decided to lower your anticipated return per year to 7 percent.

Run your eye or pencil down the 7 percent column and then across the 25-year line until you arrive at 11.6536. Divide $287,915 by 11.6536. Your answer will be $24,706.

If you earn a minimum of 7 percent from the time you are 65, you will be able to withdraw $24,706 during each of the next 25 years. Not bad for your original $15,000 investment! Aunt Martha would applaud your stewardship of her gift.

THE TAX MAN COMETH

Now you get to pay. Taxes, that is. Depending on your age, the insurance company will calculate how much of your withdrawal will be considered return of principal and how much is interest. It's obvious that if you subtracted your $15,000 from the total $287,915, you are looking at a hefty increase in income. Almost all of it will be taxed at your regular tax rate. Rest assured, it's still a good deal. With the deferral of taxes all these years, you have built up a bigger nest egg. Now that's a comforting thought.

PENALTIES, ANYONE?

Good deals rarely come without strings. Annuities are no different. If you are interested in purchasing one, you need to ask, "What penalties will the underlying company impose if I choose to withdraw some or all of my money before the deferral period is up?" Most companies have a declining or disappearing penalty charge if you withdraw before the deferral period is up. It could be 7 percent the first year, 6 percent the second, 5 percent the third, and so on. Some companies have a constant charge no matter when you withdraw.

If you buy an annuity, make sure you can withdraw a specified percentage or amount annually without penalties.

How do you find out? From the contract. Read it. Withdrawal penalties should also be clearly stated in any sales literature you've received. Most annuities do not charge you an up-front sales commission. Directly, that is. It's usually 4 percent of the total investment and is buried in the total amount. Who gets it? The broker, insurance agent or financial planner who takes your application. Is it bad? No, but it doesn't hurt to know this service isn't free. That's why there are penalties if you withdraw early. Otherwise, the insurance company figures it will make a greater profit on your money than it promised to pay you over a period of time.

If you buy an annuity, make sure you can withdraw a specified percentage or amount annually without penalties. This could vary anywhere from 5 to 10 percent a year on your original invested amount. Some even allow you to borrow from the principal amount. If you do withdraw funds before you reach the age of 59-1/2, an additional 10 percent penalty will be levied against you, plus you must declare on your tax return any amounts in excess of the monies originally placed in the annuity. Any loans made are not usually considered withdrawals, and therefore not subject to penalty.

VARIABLE ANNUITIES

Deferred annuities are fixed in their stated return or interest paid. The principal is guaranteed, and you can get your money back in seven days. A variable annuity is different. It's still an insurance contract. Neither the principal nor the rate of growth is guaranteed. If you purchase a variable annuity, you are taking on more risk than if you purchased a deferred annuity.

A variable annuity is comparable to a mutual fund. In fact, that's what it is, but there's an incentive attached. Any taxes or gains are deferred until you withdraw. The value will increase or decrease and is solely dependent upon the performance of the stock portfolio the insurance company manages. If you purchase a variable annuity, you must keep up with current stock trends. If you are bothered by market headlines of the Dow being down 20 points, for example, avoid a variable annuity. Steer toward its more conservative sister, the deferred annuity.

OTHER ADVANTAGES

Annuities offer other benefits besides deferral of taxes on gain or interest, guaranteed principal on the deferred annuity and the promise of sending your money in seven days. They can also be used as collateral; some insurance companies even have programs that enable you to borrow against your annuity. A bank will make such a loan, but it will demand physical possession of your annuity contract as collateral.

Some day you will die. Annuities avoid probate. At that time, the full value—principal plus any growth and/or interest—will be paid directly to your named beneficiary, usually without surrender or penalty charges. If you have already annuitized, selected one of the many payout options, your beneficiary will be held to the constraints of the contract. Let's say you were receiving funds under a 20-year certain payout clause and had only received monies for five years before you died. Your beneficiary would receive the same amount for the next 15 years and then no more.

Proverbs 21:20 shares, "The wise man saves for the future." And so it goes with the wise woman. An annuity can be an attractive investment option that will allow you continuity, confidence and provision for later years.

CHAPTER SIXTEEN

How to Hire the Experts

As long ago as 19 B.C., the poet Virgil was counseling "Always believe the expert." Throughout Proverbs, which Solomon began writing about the tenth century B.C., over and over he advocated the counsel of others.

Only fools refuse to be taught (1:9).

Plans go wrong with too few counselors; many counselors bring success (15:22).

Get all the advice you can and be wise the rest of your life (19:20).

Don't go to war without wise guidance; there is safety in many counselors. (24:6).

Jesus, too, taught the wisdom of working together and the apostle Paul, about A.D. 58, wrote in Romans 12:16,

"Work happily together. Don't try to act big. Don't try to get into the good graces of important people, but enjoy the company of ordinary folks. And don't think you know it all!"

In the world of money management, it is almost impossible to think you "know it all." The money game can be complex. Even after you have set specific financial goals for yourself, you need a definite strategy. Haphazard

---

It's almost inevitable that at some point you will need a bank of financial planners and consultants to keep you abreast of tax and law changes, to interpret changing interest and T-bill rates, and to give the kind of advice experts have access to and an understanding of.

---

investment won't do. In the money game particularly, the Christian advice, "Get all the advice and help you can" (See Prov. 19:20, 23:12), is both essential and relevant.

It is equally essential and relevant that Solomon advocated not just advice, but good advice, from reputable sources: "When a good man speaks, he is worth listening to, but the words of fools are a dime a dozen" (10:20).

The purpose of this chapter is not just to encourage you to seek advice from "wise men," those particular specialists and experts who can help you determine and implement a coherent, consistent financial plan appropriate for you. Certainly you can find a lot of information on your own.

There are a myriad of reliable sources, such as the *Wall Street Journal, Forbes, Barron's, Business Week, Fortune* and *Money* magazines, the *Kiplinger Tax Letter* and *Value Line Survey*.[1] There are even some good TV programs that deal intelligently with financial matters. But the truth is, you can swamp yourself with information, reading so many newspapers and magazines and survey guides that you have no time left for investing.

It's almost inevitable that at some point you will need a a bank of financial planners and consultants to keep you abreast of tax and law changes, to interpret changing interest and T-bill rates, and to give the kind of advice experts have access to and an understanding of. The old axiom, "It's not what you know but who you know," can be more appropriately restated as, "It's who you know that can contribute to what you know."

Before looking at some of the experts, keep in mind: Whoever you deal with should have been in their field of expertise for at least five years—let them make their mistakes with someone else.

THE FINANCIAL PLANNER

In starting your search for financial specialists, you might well find yourself inundated with information, confused by experts who have just the right theory for a particular moment, theories which will often conflict because they are rooted in a particular outlook or expertise. Given this, along with the complexities of today's financial arena, you may well be advised to start out with an experienced financial planner. This is a qualified professional who will act like a contractor, a general engineer who will help devise a game plan and orchestrate subcontractors who are experts in specific fields.

Another way to conceptualize the financial planner is like a general practitioner, a family doctor who will give an overall diagnosis, then refer you to the proper specialist. The planner's job is not necessarily to find the precise investment for you, but to give the best advice for your particular circumstances.

Most financial institutions—banks, insurance companies, stock brokerages and accounting firms—offer some form of personal financial management.

Planners will consult with other specialists such as attorneys, accountants and insurance brokers in order to give you a comprehensive view of your present and future financial status. Planners can contribute advice that may help you define and/or realize some of your objectives.

Most financial planners have a variety of licenses. They sell a mass of products that are available on the market. These products could include the purchase and sale of mutual funds, limited partnerships, stocks and bonds, insurance, previous metals, commodities and almost any other product that looks like it might mesh with a client's objectives.

Most financial institutions—banks, insurance companies, stock brokerages and accounting firms—offer some form of personal financial management. Often, however, their recommendations in planning are geared only to the financial substantial individual. If you don't have a lot of money for investment purposes, seek some of the independent financial services available almost anywhere. If you are unaware of them, or don't have anyone to give you a recommendation, you can contact the *Institute of Certified Financial Planners* at 3443 South Galena, Suite 190,

Denver, Colorado 80231. The ICFP consists of over 91,000 members. A directory is available that lists members. Look in your Yellow Pages under Financial Planners. This organization is comprised only of those who have completed the two-year course sponsored by the institute. However, any individual holding a CFP degree is not necessarily right for you. The degree does, though, indicate a willingness and desire to know more about tax laws and products versus just selling something to get a commission.

Your consultant should share your general financial goals and life values, giving you respect as a woman and as a Christian.

In choosing a financial planner, chemistry is one of the things to look for. There is no sense dealing with someone, no matter how competent, who gives you an uneasy feeling. Your consultant should share your general financial goals and life values, giving you respect as a woman and as a Christian. There should be some similarities in background and circumstances. And, since the client-professional union should be long-term, it would be unusual if there were any major age gap between the two of you.

Listen to recommendations from friends and acquaintances and don't be afraid to ask specific questions. You can expect your planner to be available, willing to return phone calls within the day and to spend time explaining information and recommendations to you; consistent, centered in a strategy and overview that will consider all new ideas and opportunities without becoming slave to them;

and experienced, in professional practice at least five years.

Pay attention and establish at the beginning exactly how your financial planner will be compensated. A good planner should not be a salesperson, and he or she should not earn fees solely from commissions. A fixed fee consultation plan will ensure that your planner is unbiased and available, able to give you clear professional evaluation of financial opinions.

YOUR CORPS OF SPECIALISTS

Once you have a professional financial planner, a group of financial contacts is your next goal. Investment counselors, Certified Public Accountants (CPAs), bankers, tax attorneys, etc., can provide you with information that will help you anticipate economic trends.

For example, if you had been aware that interest rates in March and April of 1980 were the highest they would be that year and would drop dramatically in the next three to four months, that information would have greatly enhanced your personal borrowing plans. Or, if you had known that throughout 1979 and the early 1980s we would experience some of the highest inflation and interest rates in years and that a recession would follow, you could have planned your purchasing and borrowing to correspond with these trends.

The key, then, is to determine and utilize the best information sources available. Specialists did not know when interest rates peaked or that we were headed for a recession. They *did* know that a combination of events creates other events.

It would be dangerous to rely on any one specialty expert, because each one comes from a particular viewpoint, with obvious limitations. Advice from parents is often awkward and probably out-of-date. Advice from other relatives and friends tends to be specialized and does not take into account that individuals are unique. Uncle Bob or Aunt Kate may be happy, successful and prosperous, but just because they used their individual talents to advantage does not mean their policies can be adopted profitably by you.

Certified Public Accountants are often very conservative. Some merely act as bookkeepers. They file tax returns and conduct audits. Financial advice should be obtained from someone who only looks forward, who considers the financial condition of the family, regardless of how they get there, and who points them in the right direction. It's okay to be conservative, but it also makes sense to be involved. If your CPA doesn't personally invest in real estate or whatever you are considering, do you think he or she can be realistic regarding the upside— or downside? Probably not.

An attorney's function concerns the law, and a banker specializes in borrowing and lending money. Few are equipped to give great advice on increasing net worth.

Stockbrokers, real estate agents and insurance agents deal with specific money products. They are usually biased in what they offer, often knowing little about options your money has in areas other than their own.

How, then, do you find professional advisors? And which will you need on a continuing basis during your lifetime? By and large, the following are some of the specialists you might use, and some of their strengths and weaknesses.

Insurance Agents

One of the first professionals you may encounter is the insurance agent. Insurance continues to go through a major revolution and will continue to do so. Insurance itself comes in all sizes and shapes. The most common is casualty—your housing contents, homeowner's, automobile, jewelry or art, medical and dental. There's also life and disability insurance. Most agents specializing in casualty will offer their clients life insurance on the side. Brokers who specialize in life and disability insurance only will often refer casualty-insurance requests to other agents, since it's a vast and complicated area. Many insurance agents have expanded into financial planning, selling mutual funds and limited partnerships.

Deal with an agent who is able to offer you rates from several different companies.

Rates and products vary substantially from company to company. Because of the competition and change within the industry, review your policies at least every three years and/or if there is a major tax law revision. Before you sign on the dotted line, make sure you fully understand its contents and limitations. Keep in mind, your needs will change as your family grows or moves away.

Bankers

Banks: We need them and they need us. Sometimes it makes sense to have more than one banker. There are times when a bank(er) is less willing to give you a loan or offer you a lower interest rate on your savings. Go next door—or tell him you will—and don't be surprised if things improve.

Your banker should not be a beginner. You want someone with some clout, who can make a decision. You do not want someone who has to ask a "higher up" for a car loan decision or to help strategize with you on your new venture. Only experience does that. You need someone who knows you, will grow with you, and who will be willing to work with you in the bad times as well as the good.

Many of us merely have a checking or a savings account and never get to know our banker. Bankers are often very flexible and willing to answer questions and offer assistance over the phone. This, of course, will be the case only after you have established a relationship with them and after they know you as an individual. Don't be afraid to approach a banker if you have minimal funds, no savings or are barely covering the bills each month. With wise financial decisions and investments that will change.

The CPA

Most of us pay taxes. Therefore one member of your team should be a good Certified Public Accountant; there are plenty of them to pick from. Your CPA needs to go beyond bookkeeping tasks. You need someone who will plan and make recommendations that are appropriate for you no matter where you are. Many accountants specialize in specific areas—small businesses, real estate, tax exempt organizations—so find out if yours does. If 90 percent of their business is in the medical field and you are a teacher, a match might not be made.

When you interview accountants, make sure you ask how they are compensated, what their areas of expertise are and what their tax saving track records are for previous clients. Ask if any of their clients are audited or get large refunds. If a high percentage are audited, does it mean the CPA is too aggressive, interpreting the tax laws very loosely, or does it mean that the majority of the clientele is part of a high audit area, such as doctors and dentists? If refunds are hefty, how come? Withholding should be changed to reflect a decrease in tax obligation each year. A CPA should query you as to your anticipated income, determine what expenses could be tax deductible and advise you of appropriate W-4 changes.

Tax laws change constantly, so it's important to deal with a professional who not only keeps up with such changes but is alert to any advantages that may result to his clients.

One final suggestion. Ask your accountant if she will stand by you in the case of an audit and/or appear in your behalf.

Remuneration for this member of your cast is usually billed on an hourly basis plus computer costs if applicable.

The Tax Attorney

If you've had any large windfalls, or have made a significant amount of money, you would be well-advised to consult a tax attorney. Tax attorneys combine a knowledge of law with the expertise of an accountant. They are expensive, are not right for most of us, but are certainly there if the need should ever arise.

Tax attorneys, as do other attorneys, charge for their time by the hour. They will also charge for all phone calls, paperwork, copying, etc. Be organized when dealing with them, otherwise your bills will mushroom.

The Stockbroker

When you buy or sell stocks and bonds, you use a stockbroker. As in the case of insurance, the securities industry has gone through a substantial revolution over the last decade. Stockbrokers sell just about everything: tax shelters, insurance, annuities, commodities, options.

Some specialize in specific industries. A friend of mine is recognized as one of the top experts in the technology area. Any time I consult with a client who is interested in technology-related companies, I refer them directly to him.

Other brokers only recite what their firm produces in investment recommendations. If you follow the tips in chapter 6 on identifying trends, you can make many stock purchasing decisions on your own.

Stockbrokers get paid by commission. If you work with a broker who is with a full service brokerage—like Merrill Lynch or Dean Witter—and you constantly ask questions or demand service but rarely buy or sell anything, your broker may soon lose interest in you.

If you aren't interested in advice, use a discount brokerage house—one that offers reduced commission to its customers when they buy and sell securities. Charles Schwab and Company was rated the #1 brokerage house a few years ago. Why? Because their services were better, at least according to the general public. Discount houses provide the same insurance coverage on your accounts as the full-service companies. The primary difference is you are not inundated with all kinds of investment recommendations. Savings on commissions will be approximately 50 percent.

Real Estate Brokers

If you are considering making a commercial real estate investment—apartments, office buildings—deal with someone who has considerable experience in real estate, specifically in the commercial field. An agent or broker who specializes in residential property is very different from the commercial broker. Raw land purchases should be made through an agent or broker who knows the area and the nuances of buying raw land. And there's more. Real estate is bought and sold in a variety of ways and in a variety of packages. Each has different tax consequences as well as financing requirements. Look before you leap, and understand what can go wrong, before it does.

Property Managers

If you own or are a partner in complexes such as apartment buildings, it may make sense to hire professional management. Many say they know how to manage property, but it's indeed an art that demands years of experience and know-how. There are firms both large and small handling complexes ranging in size from a few units to thousands. They can be very efficient because they spread their overhead costs and often have extensive computer resources. As a result, ongoing income and expense statements are available. You can keep up-to-date on your property, noting any irregularities as they arise.

Specialists as Resources

Unfortunately, in this day and age, it is no longer enough to be a "good and thrifty individual." Since you have come this far in establishing financial objectives and developing financial savvy, it would be foolish not to use all the available sources to monitor and implement your strategy.

Specialists are no replacement for your own hard-won understanding and autonomous financial control. But you still need the help of those who know their way through the maze of laws and regulations and the intricacies and refinements that mark today's financial, legal and tax worlds. "The advice of a wise man refreshes like water from a mountain spring. Those accepting it become aware of the pitfalls on ahead" (Prov. 13:14).

Note
1. The majority of these publications may be purchased at your local newsstand, except for *Value Line Survey,* which may be obtained from any brokerage, library or by writing *Value Line Survey,* Arnold Bernhard & Co., Inc., 711 Third Ave., New York, NY 10017.

CHAPTER SEVENTEEN
Putting It All Together

There's an old fable often used by church vestries seeking to collect annual pledges. It concerns Satan who is interviewing three apprentice devils about to go into the world to ply their trade.

"I'm going to tell people there's no God," says the first.

"Well," responds Satan, "you probably won't convince many people. No matter what you say, most are already convinced that there is a God."

"I'm going to tell people that there's no hell," states the second. "Well," responds Satan, "you might be surprised. Most people already know that there is a hell."

"I'm going to tell people that there's no hurry," says the third.

"Well," responds Satan, "you will certainly be very successful!"

DON'T PUT IT OFF

Don't let procrastination get in the way of realizing your financial capabilities. You have come this far seeking the motivation and methods for developing your own financial plan. Don't stop now. Don't put off its implementation with excuses, or you'll look up five years from now shaking your head, lamenting, "Why didn't I do it sooner?"

Financial savvy is constantly responding to changing laws, changing economic factors and changing money values—inflation. You must have the tenacity and experience to flow with these changes and turn them to your advantage.

I feel justified in including this admonition, because I fear many of you thought you were going to get through this book and emerge with a working financial plan, a definitive directive for financial success. Instead, you have emerged with information and tools to forge your own plan.

There are absolute ground rules for how much of your net worth or investable monies you should put in any particular type of investment. There are some advisors who will draw charts or graphs or even pyramids to indicate a certain percent should be allotted to high-risk, a certain percent to growth and a certain percent to conservative investments.

While diversification is advisable, every woman will have a different degree of risk-taking ability. One of my clients was in her 60s and loved the action of the commodity markets. She was bored by utility stocks that might produce attractive dividends. Another had a substantial seven-figure net worth—most of it inherited—who would never consider anything riskier than a bond or a certificate of deposit.

All of us are different. We are all seeking to meet varying objectives and we all have varying degrees of risks that we are willing to take to do so. Your objectives and goals must be reachable for you, and your methods must be aligned with your own interests and instincts.

Besides having no definitive formula, financial planning is evolutionary. Christian faith is based on fixed beliefs and principles. "Jesus Christ is the same yesterday, today, and forever." (Heb. 13:8). But financial savvy is constantly responding to changing laws, changing economic factors and changing money values—inflation. You must have the tenacity and experience to flow with these changes and turn them to your advantage. Your hope for a successful financial future depends upon your ability to educate yourself in life, set goals, be resilient when you make mistakes and learn from them.

Financial savvy must also respond to changing personal circumstances. The strategy you choose will be a part of your life and as such, will be affected by, and ought to include, life's changing phases, its upsets, its catastrophes, its serendipities.

More and more, I am seeing both single and married Christian women becoming more actively involved in investments, overviews, objectives and the everyday nuances of money. Those of you who are fortunate enough to have substantial investable assets can select different opportunities attractive to you. Even if you have large sums available, you may choose to pool your dollars with others' simply as a means of diversifying and spreading the risk around.

Married couples often choose to keep their funds separate, allowing each individual to select his or her own investments. Some couples even enjoy competing with each other to see how well they can do. More often than not in these situations, I have found that the woman sur-

---

Financial savvy will enable you to produce your financial plan, which will then become your vehicle for making the materials you care for, whatever they may be, more abundant in your life.

---

prises both herself and her partner as she sees how fast she is learning and how apt her instincts are. By researching your options and assessing your own resources and talents and tastes, the possibilities are endless.

BE WILLING TO WORK AT IT

Because money management has no fixed answers and no fixed circumstances, it will require a good deal of time, hard work and energy. The Bible tells us that hard work is a virtue—"Hard work means prosperity; only a fool idles away his time," shares Proverbs 12:11. It also alerts us to the value of patience in money and investments—"An inheritance quickly gained . . . will not be blessed at the end," forewarns Proverbs 20:21 (*NIV*).

If you attempt too much too quickly and expect that everything you do will work perfectly the first time, you may be in for some disappointments and surprises. It's necessary to keep working to reach your goal. As I have told client after client, class after class, you will certainly make mistakes, but by diversifying and always asking questions, you can learn to minimize your losses and maximize your capacity as an effective, informed investor.

NOW IT'S UP TO YOU!

This book will help you devise a coherent, consistent financial plan. But you are the one who must finalize it and implement it. "Work brings profit; talk brings poverty!" Proverbs 14:23 forecasts.

Financial savvy will enable you to produce your financial plan, which will then become your vehicle for making the materials you care for, whatever they may be, more abundant in your life. "Wealth from gambling quickly disappears; wealth from hard work grows," should become one of your rules to live by, as Proverbs 13:11 illustrates.

"A wise woman builds her house, while a foolish woman tears hers down by her own efforts," warns Proverbs 14:1. You can build your house through sound financial management. You can tear it down with procrastination and excuses. The rewards for having and using your own financial savvy are immense. In the end, they will give you the kind of freedom and security that is fast becoming every woman's—and every Christian's—birthright.

Epilogue

From 1980 to 1990, the gurus of Wall Street have introduced over 600 new "investment" opportunities for the consumer—you. Hindsight, being what it is, shows that most didn't make their mark. Instead, the consumer's expectations were never met—most of these "opportunities" turned into financial disasters.

The past decade will go down in the history books as the one infiltrated with greed and "me-ism." The rush of so many of us to stretch far more than what was necessary, to attempt a "quick fix" to our financial problems and to jump into areas that we really didn't understand are reflections of the decade.

When it comes to money and taxes, the only constant is and will be change. In this revised edition of *The Money Guide for Christian Women,* all tax changes have been reflected through 1990. For your financial and tax health, it is critical to keep abreast of any changes that may affect you—from retirement contributions to IRAs, KEOGHs,

401(k) programs and any of the new breed that are guaranteed to surface in the 1990s.

The strength and beauty of *The Money Guide for Christian Women* is that it is loaded with common sense— not a zillion methods and ways to make a dollar and avoid taxes. I have emphasized strategies that have been around for a long time, that have been proven by others and that are understandable. The last thing that an investor/ consumer needs is a Ph.D. in legalese, statistics, returns or opportunities. What is needed is a Ph.D. in Life, recognizing that mistakes will be made, and that when they come they become learning modules for future reference.

Proverbs 19:20 reminds each of us to "Get all the advice you can and be wise the rest of your life." Wise words that have lived for generations—the past, the present and the future.

JUDITH BRILES
7792 East Iowa St.
Denver, CO 80231
303-745-4590
Winter, 1991

Index